THE MINISTRY OF THE FAT

Unveiling Our New Identity In Christ

HEATHER THOMPSON

Therefore, if anyone is in Christ, he is a new creation, old things have passed away; behold, all things have become new
2 Corinthians 5:17

Dedication

Dedicated to Jim Hagan who was a true friend and encourager to all.

Publisher's statement: Throughout this book, the love for our God is such that whenever we refer to
Him, we honour with capitals. On the other hand, when referring to the devil, we refuse to acknowledge
him with any honour to the point of violating grammatical rule and withholding capitalisation.

Published by

Maurice Wylie Media
Inspirational Christian Publisher

For more information visit
www.MauriceWylieMedia.com

Endorsement

"A Journey of Discovery" is exactly what you continue to experience when you read this book! As you travel through the pages you discover that Heather is introducing the reader further to the ministry of the Father's heart which is clearly Freedom! The book is saturated in Scripture and brimming with advice that is biblical and offers a pathway to healing, wholeness and restoration. Every page reflects the author's love for God, a deep maturity in Christ and a passion to see the captives set free in Jesus' Name!

Rev Dr Colin Dickson BD, DipMin, MTh, D.Min
(Bachelor of Divinity, Postgraduate Diploma in Ministry, Master of Theology, Doctor of Ministry)

Contents

Foreword

In the series of three books which Heather has written this is the second volume. In the first book there are spiritual insights that lead us into the presence of God resulting in spiritual enrichment and blessing. If you haven't read volume one, I strongly recommend it.

The Christian whose life is truly dedicated to the Lord Jesus Christ longs to experience that more abundant life that we find through being in Christ and yet at times we seem to fall short of it. In this second book Heather directs us towards two further ways through which we can enter into a greater fullness of life.

In the first section entitled, "Inner Strength" we who are in Christ are encouraged to explore the attributes that God our Father has deposited within our spirits from creation and which are readily available to us to strengthen us in our daily lives.

His love enables us to love those we may find difficult to love without fear of the cost.

Our hope is Jesus and His sacrifice on our behalf. It is sure and steady lighting up the path ahead. In the darkest night we can reach out and touch the hem of His garment, "If God is for us who can be against us." How wonderful to know we are under the shelter of His wings.

There may be times when we are uncertain and have doubts. Doubt is completely different to unbelief which is a refusal to believe. Doubt is seeking the truth. When we listen to the voice of faith in our spirits we are reassured and strengthened to believe. In this section Heather gives illustrations of how God spoke to her giving her guidance, protection and security. She then discusses how we can experience the life of God that is resident within us, receiving His wisdom and enjoying companionship with Him day by day, truly a blessing and encouragement.

In the second section, Our Victory in Christ Jesus, Heather writes about the practical issues involved in the Ministry of Healing and Deliverance giving many helpful illustrations. There is good, wise and sound guidance as the result of many years of Spirit-led and guided ministry. This is a book we will return to again and again because there is in-depth teaching on names of demonic powers, their purpose and activity, and how the Lord Jesus Christ breaks their hold, influence and power setting the captives free, just as Jesus said, "I have come to set the captives free". There is teaching on the influences of curses and ancestral spirits which have been passed down the generational line.

Through reading this book the oppressed and discouraged will discover there is hope, that there is a way to freedom, and that they can enjoy life in all its fullness just as Jesus said. Here we also have a most valuable resource for those seeking to bring help and wholeness to the oppressed. Truly this is a Spirit-inspired book assuring us that greater is He who is for us than he who is against us. We will return to it again and again.

Rev. Jim Hagan
Minister Emeritus,
Donacloney Presbyterian Church, Lurgan, Northern Ireland.

Introduction

In the first book, *A Journey of Discovery,*[1] we reflected on who God is, all-powerful, all- knowing, without beginning or end - "I Am That I Am".[2] We thought about His purpose in creating us, that we might have a close relationship as a child of our loving Heavenly Father. We learnt that, because our sin separates us from this possibility, such a relationship only becomes possible through trusting in Jesus Christ who paid the price for our sin, taking it upon Himself when He was crucified.[3] He is the Way to the Father – the only way in which we can be reconciled to Holy God and so live in eternity with Him.[4] Referring to various scriptures, we learnt who the Holy Spirit is and how He helps us throughout our lives. We faced our need of repentance and forgiveness and touched on two aspects of healing: emotional and physical. Finally, we explored the joy of being able to have conversations with God our heavenly Father.

The journey continues…

When we become a new creation, we discover that God has equipped us in many different ways for an exciting, fulfilling life with Him. In the first book we discussed the important role that the Spirit of God plays in our daily lives: guiding our prayers and enabling us to

---

1   A Journey of Discovery by Heather Thompson, 2022, published by Maurice Wylie Media.
2   Exodus 3:7-8, 13-14.
3   Romans 6:23; 2 Corinthians 5:21.
4   John 14:6.

hear God's voice, encouraging and strengthening us, convicting us of sinful attitudes and actions, releasing His gifts to build up the Body of Christ. In this book in the first section, *Inner Strength*, we will be exploring the spiritual attributes of God which are resident within our renewed spirits because of the indwelling Spirit of God. These equip and strengthen us for our journey throughout life.

Although we can determine to stop participating in what we know to be wrong and pray earnestly for freedom we may find ourselves remaining captive in some way, e.g., to emotional outbursts or addictions. We may sense that deep within something is not right, or struggle with strange dreams or fragments of unpleasant memories. Possibly, unknown to us, we are being tormented by an adverse evil spirit or are suffering from the consequences of past trauma. In the second section, *Our Victory in Christ Jesus*, we will be considering the destructive influence of evil spirits. In the third book we will explore different ways in which past traumas can affect us.

While praying one day I had a vision of Jesus hanging on the Cross suffering. Wave after wave of sin and sickness was assaulting Him. The scene then changed to one in which my attention was drawn to an ornate bird cage with the door locked and a woman standing beside it with a key in her hand. As I pondered what this all meant the word "freedom" surfaced from my spirit and, somehow, I "knew" that the Holy Spirit was showing me that the locked cage symbolised the fact that Jesus voluntarily gave up His freedom[5] for us. He was totally imprisoned by the evil of the flesh, the world and the devil and experienced the judgements of God. Separated from His Father, He called out in agony of mind and heart, body and spirit. In choosing to lose His freedom He was making it possible for us to gain ours,

---

5   John 10:17,18.

Since the children have flesh and blood, he too shared in their humanity so that by his death he might break the power of him who holds the power of death — that is, the devil — and free those who all their lives were held in slavery by their fear of death. Hebrews 2:14-15

I asked, "Why is a woman holding the key, Lord?" Two thoughts came,

- the woman represents "wisdom". In Proverbs 1:20 wisdom is referred to as female, "*she raises her voice*". In His wisdom God in Christ Jesus chose this way to reconcile us to Him.

- "keeper of the key". When, in the Garden of Eden, we chose to listen to satan rather than obey God because we wanted knowledge independently of Him, we turned our back on His gift of revelation through which He communicates with us. God is restoring this gift of revelation to us. This is explained in this book, where reference is made to "*keeper of the key*"[6].

As we abide in Christ, exploring and applying the truths in God's Word, we will soar in freedom, knowing our true identity in Christ.

The first section in this book unveils aspects of our true identity in Christ of which we may not be aware, the divine attributes that God has restored to us when we were born again. In Christ we are so much more powerful than we may realise. The second section unveils how, as an aspect of our new identity, God has raised us up with Christ and seated us with him in the heavenly realms in Christ Jesus, far above all rule and authority, power and dominion. It is from there that we use our authority in the name of Jesus against the wiles of the enemy so as to live in freedom.

---

6   A Journey of Discovery by Heather Thompson, 2022, published by Maurice Wylie Media. Section 1.1 p53

SECTION 1

INNER STRENGTH

"I pray that out of his glorious riches he may strengthen you with power through his Spirit in your inner being."

Ephesians 3:16

Chapter 1.1
Attributes of the Spirit

"The thief comes only to steal and kill and destroy;
I have come that they may have life and have it to the full."
John 10:10b

Sometimes we may wonder whether we are really experiencing the abundant life that Jesus promises and we may conclude that there is more that we can enter into if we ask ourselves some questions,

- Is our *faith* consistently strong, speaking words of truth into our hearts and minds?

- Do we have an unshakeable *love* that will love those we find it impossible to like or trust?

- Do we have a burning, unwavering *hope* that is firmly placed in Jesus and not in what He might or might not do for us?

- Do we experience *life* within, bubbling up ceaselessly in thanksgiving, praise and worship of God?

- Do we regularly and freely receive *revelation* from God?

- Do we experience God's *wisdom* as a frequent occurrence?

- Do we enjoy *companionship* with God our Father, as Adam and Eve did before they were excluded from the Garden of Eden?

God wants us to be able to say, "Yes", to each of the above questions but, so often, we cannot. We struggle and doubt and blame ourselves because we do not experience all that we expect from reading the promises and teachings in scripture. We may know that Jesus is our Peace, our Shepherd, our Provider, our Banner of Love and that He is always present with us. Somehow, it can also be true that at times our lives appear to be devoid of the evidence for these.

So far, on this journey of healing, we have discussed the ongoing need for repentance, forgiveness and inner healing. We turn now to explore the fullness, the abundance that is ours through recognising the potential within our spirits, the gifts of God to us from creation which lie dormant until we are born anew.

Earlier, as we reflected upon God's invitation to fellowship with Him through two-way communication (Book 1), we began a journey into nurturing such fruitfulness in our inner lives. Such a relationship gradually releases revelation of how much God loves us and, through becoming convinced of this deep within, brings us into complete security in Jesus. I want, now, to take you with me on the next part of my journey towards this.

As we continue to grow in our relationship with God we come to understand and receive more of the riches of His grace towards us who are in Christ. In this section I would like to describe how God my Father opened up my understanding to a further restoration, this time towards greater awareness of the fullness of His attributes within my spirit. As I travelled this road with God, I was able to move into more consistency in receiving revelation and wisdom from Him, and into discovering inner strength through recognising the steady confidence of His faith and love within me. Along with this is the hope within that looks unwaveringly to Jesus, and which leads to a life full of worship. Thus, I began to experience what abundant life really can be.

Since we are all created in the image of God who is Spirit,[7] we have all the attributes of God's Spirit resident within our spirits, but the full potential arising from this is denied us through being part of a fallen race. When we become Christians, our spirits are renewed but, even then, we may walk through much of the Christian life without being aware of the full potential that God has placed within us and so, as a consequence, live at a lower level of spiritual engagement than we could. Each attribute of God's Holy Spirit may be active to some extent but, as we follow God's leading, we can be released in a greater way in each. I believe that what I am about to share is a deeper work of the Holy Spirit which God leads us into through our having an ongoing and intimate relationship with Jesus. This part of my story describes how I was led into understanding this awakening to the potential within my spirit that now enables me to connect more readily with God's heart and will.

As God unfolded this revelation to me, He focussed on seven of His attributes within my spirit: hope, love, faith, life, wisdom, revelation, companionship. These are not the only attributes of the Spirit of God. Threaded throughout scripture many aspects of the Spirit are revealed.

He is the Spirit of Truth — John 15:26; 16:13; 1 John. 4:6.
The Spirit of Power, Love, and Self-Discipline — 2 Timothy 1:7.
The Spirit of Wisdom — Deuteronomy 34:9; Proverbs 1:23.
The Spirit of Judgement — Isaiah 4:4; 19:4; 29:10.
The Spirit of Life — Revelation 11:11.
The Spirit of Justice and Mercy — Isaiah 11:1-3.

---

7   John 4:24.

The seven aspects of His Spirit that God had chosen to instruct me on at this stage are mentioned in Paul's prayers to the Colossian and Ephesian churches (Colossians 1; Ephesians 1,3).

Our spirits are untainted by our thoughts and emotions and so are pure channels of God's grace and love. Our spirit man is complete in Christ,

> *"and you are complete in Him, who is the head of all principality and power."* Colossians 2:10 NKJV

Because our minds are prone to thinking and deducing independently of God, they need to be brought into alignment with the mind of Christ through studying the Word of God. Only then will we have true agreement between our souls and spirits. These attributes all have the potential of increasing in fullness within us as we live our lives in the light of Jesus and move towards greater obedience and restoration,

> *"And we all, with unveiled face, beholding the glory of the Lord, are being transformed into the same image from one degree of glory to another. For this comes from the Lord who is the Spirit."* 2 Corinthians 3:18

Since we are in Christ, here in this life we are being restored into confident hope and trust in God, having His knowledge and wisdom and experiencing His unwavering love, all so that we can live in companionship with Him. This restoration will be consummated when we meet with Him face to face.

Is it necessary to know about different attributes of the Spirit in our spirits? Is He not one Spirit? When scripture speaks about the Spirit of wisdom and understanding, the Spirit of counsel and strength, the Spirit of knowledge and fear of the Lord,[8] the Spirit is not being split

---

8   Isaiah 11:2.

into parts but, rather, God is revealing various aspects of the Holy Spirit. When we learn something new it is often broken down into small pieces to make understanding and learning easier. In discussing the various attributes of God within our spirits, we are highlighting just how amazing it is that God in His fullness dwells within us and is helping us become more fully aware of His resources within. Then, as we become practiced in being alert to each attribute, we become consistently alert to what God is saying to us. There comes a point where we don't always think, "oh, this is coming from faith in my spirit" or "this is coming from revelation in my spirit." It is all coming from the one Spirit of God and being relayed through our spirits. But there will be times when knowing specifically that we believe a certain thing from the depths of our being gives confidence and reassurance that we are moving in faith. At other times we may receive information from our spirit and think, "I never knew that", and realize that spirit revelation has spoken. Let's not get hung up on the detail but use any revelation that comes to us as a steppingstone towards strengthening our spiritual lives.

Christ's Kingdom is of a spiritual nature and administered in a spiritual manner. The Spirit within us and upon us releases faith, revelation etc. The seven aspects of His Spirit that God chose to teach us about are mentioned within the following passage,

> *"In Him also we have obtained an inheritance, being predestined according to the purpose of Him who works all things according to the counsel of His will, that we who first trusted in Christ should be to the praise of His glory. In Him you also trusted, after you heard the word of truth, the gospel of your salvation; in whom also, having believed, you were sealed with the Holy Spirit of promise, who is the guarantee of our inheritance until the redemption of the purchased possession, to the praise of His glory (life). Therefore I also, after I heard of your faith in the Lord Jesus and your love for all the saints, do not cease to give thanks for you, making mention*

of you in my prayers: that the God of our Lord Jesus Christ, our Father God of glory, may give to you the spirit of wisdom and revelation in the knowledge of Him, the eyes of your understanding being enlightened; that you may know what is the hope of His calling, what are the riches of the glory of His inheritance in the saints (companionship), and what is the exceeding greatness of His power toward us who believe, according to the working of His mighty power." Ephesians 1:11-19

Knowing that we have these attributes of the Spirit within our spirits increases our wonder at how gracious God is to us. Through the Spirit, we can know in our spirits what surpasses human knowledge. The primary purpose is so that we can know the love of God and His ways of love,

"For this reason, I kneel before our Father God, from whom every family in heaven and on earth derives its name. I pray that out of His glorious riches He may strengthen you with power through His Spirit in your inner being, so that Christ may dwell in your hearts through faith. And I pray that you, being rooted and established in love, may have power, together with all God's people, to grasp how wide and long and high and deep is the love of Christ, and to know this love that surpasses knowledge – that you may be filled to the measure of all the fullness of Christ." Ephesians 3:14-19

In the third book of the series, *The Ministry of the Father's Heart*, I will describe how God used insights arising from these attributes in my spirit along with confirmation through His Word to lead me into a deep personal conviction of His love, love that gave me security.

For Meditation

"Is anyone thirsty? Come and drink." Isaiah 55:1 NLT

"For I will pour out water to quench your thirst and to irrigate your parched fields." Isaiah 44:3 NLT

"The Lord will guide you continually, giving you water when you are dry, and restoring your strength." Isaiah 58:11 NLT

"Then the angel showed me the water of life, clear as crystal, flowing from the throne of God and of the Lamb." Revelation 22:1 NLT

"Anyone who is thirsty may come to Me. Anyone who believes in Me may come and drink! For the scriptures declare, 'Rivers of living water will flow from his belly/heart/innermost being.'" John 7:37-38 NLT

Or, according to the Passion Translation,

"All of you thirsty ones, come to Me! Come to Me and drink! Believe in Me, so that rivers of living water will burst out from within you; flowing from your innermost being, just like the scripture says, 'rivers of living water will flow from His throne within.'" John 7:37-38 TPT

Chapter 1.2

Awakening to the Love of God Within

"For the Spirit God gave us does not make us timid,
but gives us power, love and self-discipline."
2 Timothy 1:7

When God taught us about the attributes of the Holy Spirit within our spirits, He began by giving further revelation about His love. What we came to describe as "spirit love" was essentially a reflection of the pure love of our Father God which is resident within our spirits. Because we are each made in the image of God, we all have this love in us from creation but it may remain dormant until awakened at an appointed time. The supreme example of this kind of love was shown by Jesus as He hung on the cross. He demonstrated love that was resolute in the face of temptation, unflinching in the face of pain, that forgave those responsible for His crucifixion and that offered life to a people heading for death. It was the love of God in all its purity.

Some think that if the Church has anything to do with people who are outcasts or evil in some way that it will become polluted but it won't. The Church stands out as different. It is to people what they need, whether it be peace or love, whether it be forgiveness or joy. Jesus wants us, His Church, to go in His name into the world to bring life to the lost and hurting, and not be afraid that we will be ineffective.

We are to bring the light of Jesus into the darkness. Recently, I was reading a book by Blake Healy,[9] a man who frequently sees in the spirit. On one occasion when he was sixteen and part of the Youth Group in his church, he was spending an afternoon in a nearby area wandering past stall after stall where people were offering free psychic readings, doomsday prophecies, and handmade jewellery. Many of the people milling around were on drugs or deep into the occult but were open to hearing the Good News of Jesus Christ because they had come to the realization that they were in need of something better. As the author wandered with his friends, he heard God tell him to look back to where they had been walking. When He did so, he saw a pathway of light all along the route that they had taken. This church youth group was bringing the light of Christ wherever they went. He concludes, "The light that followed us wasn't something special that one time on that day. When you're a child of God, you change everything you touch". The church brings life to the world. The world needs to hear that Jesus is alive.

Over the years we have received many insights from God for our church. Three of these have a bearing on what I have written above: the Church as a filling station where people come to be filled with the Holy Spirit and be restored, healed and set free in some way, the Church as a hospital ward with many beds, again depicting a place of welcome, restoration and healing, and the Church as a ship carrying goods out all over the world.

When we invite Jesus into our lives and ask Him to fill us with His Spirit, we enter into a new life in Him. As we obey His teaching, aligning our minds with the mind of Christ we discover that it is His love in our hearts that reaches out and encourages those around us. There will be times when we choose to love even when we find it difficult because that is what Jesus wants, and because He offers us His

---

9   The Veil, An invitation to the Unseen Realm pp 37-41 by Blake Healy, Charisma House, 2018.

grace when we obey. This is genuine agape love, unconditional love which wants the best for the person. As we live a life of love, reaching out to one another with selfless love, we become freer from our own selfish desires, and ultimately from the fear of the cost to ourselves. However, like the part of an iceberg above the surface, this love is only a fraction of what we have the potential to offer. There will be times when, although we want to reach out in love, we find it difficult for many different reasons, maybe on occasion being hampered by our own bigotries and by attitudes of the moment that arise out of belief systems in our hearts. God our Father can help us.

Love of God

As we continue to walk in love, we discover that there is a deeper source of love which, like the submerged part of the iceberg, is extensive. This deeper source of love is resident in our spirits and is an attribute of God.

This love in our spirits is a deeper steadier love than what we already experience in our hearts as Christians in that it is not diminished in action by our fleshly weaknesses.

It is our Father God's love in all its purity and cannot be tainted by our buried emotions or by our limited thinking. Once we invite Jesus into our lives it can rise up from within our spirits even when we ourselves can't muster up the desire to love from our hearts. It is a force rather than a feeling, a force of love resident in our spirit and awakened by our Heavenly Father.

As God does not overrule our freedom to choose, this love only operates freely in those who have a lifestyle of choosing to love, who want to be like Jesus, and are in a place where God knows He would be given freedom to release His love. It is strong and propels the person into welcoming and loving another whom, previously, they may not have been able to, and because it is the desired thing to do. The person offering this love is secure,

"rooted and established in love." Ephesians 3:17

and not fearful of the consequences of being affected adversely by the other because the One who initiates it is reliable and trustworthy,

"There is no fear in love. But perfect love casts out fear." 1 John 4:18

There can be no thought of revenge in a person through whom this love manifests. It enables a person truly to love one who has offended them deeply, for example, one who has been abused finding that they are able to release this love towards the abuser and so touch them with God's healing. Such love in a person draws them into "climbing over the fence" and sitting beside the one needing love. There is no separation in thought or heart and no sense of other but, rather, a God-given ability to touch the other person with the complete acceptance and love of our Father God.

This love is a supernatural force of love, and has within it the ability to show the repentant, the wicked, or the evil person that God has a place in His heart for them, and that God's people will receive them. It is a love that overcomes rejection, fear and mistrust and is especially significant for those whose trust has been betrayed. It seems that the presence of this love in one person can touch another with such purity and truth that the recipient immediately is enabled to trust the one who reaches out to them. It is God's love and brings healing in its wings.

It is not a love that grows within us but one which reaches out from our spirits at our Father God's bidding. Love that is a fruit of the Holy Spirit is the love of Jesus which is birthed within us when we receive Jesus into our lives, and which grows as we walk with, and in obedience to, Him. The love issuing from our spirits is within us waiting until the time when our Father God awakens it because it has a specific role to play,

"Do not arouse or awaken love until it so desires."
Song of Solomon 8:4

Once awakened, it is available for God our Father to initiate from within us at any time.

My first awareness of this amazing attribute came one morning when I experienced what felt like a punch in my spirit and immediately thought, "what's that?" I felt love rising up from my spirit and a desire to reach out and comfort the person beside me. It was as though something or someone other than me was initiating this love in me for the person. Later I understood that this someone was God, my heavenly Father. The original drive/force that I felt had occurred when God my Father had awakened His love that had been resident within my spirit. It triggered off a depth of unconditional love which, for whatever reason, I had not been feeling for this person up until then.

On a different occasion, I was in the presence of an alcoholic who had taken too many drinks and was acting silly. I could feel no compassion for her even though I tried. I called on God to release His love through me. I watched as others laughed and talked with her, all the time feeling self-condemnatory. Later, I asked God why I wasn't able to reach out with His love and was told, "I didn't prompt you to. I didn't release My love through you at that time." God is love and loves every person all of the time, so why had He not released His love through me? Sometimes, it is difficult to understand why God does what He does and we have to trust Him that He knows best. I came to the conclusion that this specific love of our Father God is only released by Him as and when He chooses, and that this could be a safeguard within the Body of Christ because only He knows what is going on in a person's heart. Only He knows where there is the potential for true repentance and a desire to change. It is not that He withholds His love but that He wants us to listen to His promptings because He knows what is best for all. He is full of compassion, but He does not encourage wrong behaviour.

Since we are made in the image of God we have the potential for this love from conception, but because we are born in sin and into a fallen world it remains dormant until after we invite Jesus into our lives. From then on, we have the potential to be filled with the Holy Spirit and to be fully awakened to this love of God and enjoy companionship with Him. We see this love consistently demonstrated by Jesus because He did not inherit the consequences of sinful nature and was without sin. He lived in the fullness of this love of the Father.

Once we understand that, through being born again, the Spirit of God and of Jesus comes to live within, then we have a choice to allow the Spirit freedom in our lives or to restrict Him. Without this understanding, we may limit God through limiting His Spirit, even if unintentionally. Once a person yields to the Holy Spirit, their life changes and their desire to get to know Jesus more and more and to serve Him grows.

God is awakening this love in the Church, restoring her to being Christ-like, loving with His love and revealing His heart for a lost world through demonstrations of the power of His Holy Spirit. The Church is being revived, and as outsiders look on, they will see a people living radically different to the world,

"By this everyone will know that you are my disciples, if you love one another." John 13:34-35

Imagine a church in which all were willing to move with this pure love of our Father God. Every contact with a seeker, however hurt or abused, would draw that person in without fear of the cost to themselves or the fellowship, and would enable the same pure love to be awakened in that person. Imagine a church where an abuser would be welcomed with that kind of love even while recognizing the awfulness of the crime that they had committed. Consider how we would react to a paedophile coming to our church. Would we not be full of fear and protective of our children? How would we be able to love unconditionally? How would we know whether professed repentance was true or a guise for infiltrating a vulnerable group? Since this force of love comes from our Father God, we can be sure that He will not initiate it unless He thinks it best. We can trust Him to give us discernment so that we stay on His path.

God is preparing the Church for times of hardship. With such love the Church will be secure and stand fearlessly. Individuals will have love that cries out, "Father, forgive them for they know not what they do", and grace to love the very people who are abusing them.

The awakening of this love enables deep spirit to Spirit communion with our Father God without the need for words, and an understanding of what He is doing so that we can, as Jesus did, be doing what our Father God is doing.

Once I had been awakened to the fact that I had this love in my spirit, the Holy Spirit said to me, "Now, go and read the Bible and you will know a difference". I found this to be true. As I read, I seemed to receive revelation of Jesus more readily, and was given insights on a much more regular basis. I was now reading through the eyes of one who was secure in God's love, and who was communing with Him moment by moment while He spoke revelation to me through His word in a truly life-giving way. He truly is the,

"Revealer of mysteries." Daniel 2:47

God freely gives revelation to those who will receive and use it under the umbrella of His love.

May God bless you as you seek His face for all that He wants to release through you.

Chapter 1.3

Awakening to the Hope of God Within

"We have this hope as an anchor for the soul,
firm and secure."
Hebrews 6:19

No matter what assails us we have a sure and certain hope, a hope that is placed in Jesus. Our struggle to keep our eyes on this hope is sourced in our distressing feelings and negative thoughts, in the stresses and pressures which at times can overwhelm us, and although these cannot undo what Jesus has done for us, we can lose sight of that truth in the turmoil. Even when we wonder whether God is there for us at all, the truth is that He is close by and walking through the difficulty with us. He tells us,

"I will make you strong. I will help you." Isaiah 41:10 GN

Jesus is our example,

"For the joy set before him he endured the cross, scorning its shame, and sat down at the right hand of the throne of God. Consider him who endured such opposition from sinners, so that you will not grow weary and lose heart." Hebrews 12:2b-3

His hope was in the joy of knowing that the outcome of His suffering and resurrection would be victory on our behalf and would enable companionship with those whom He had created. When we are suffering, we have hope as a focus, the sure and certain hope that is founded in Jesus and which assures us that there will always be a resurrection,

> *"fixing our eyes on Jesus, the pioneer and perfecter of faith."*
> Hebrews 12:2a

Sometimes our hope is placed on positive outcomes like success, healing, or meaningful relationships, but hopes such as these can be dashed because they have originated in our minds or emotions, or are dependent on circumstances or people. We frequently place our hope in the seed of the promise rather than in the source of the promise. Hope placed in anything other than Jesus is not Biblical Hope i.e.,

> *"In Christ alone my hope is found...all other ground is sinking sand".*[10]

This hope is sure and certain, and founded on Jesus' sacrifice and resurrection. Purity of hope is released within us as an attribute of God, rising up from within our spirits. When God is giving us the ability to hope it is because we are seeing from God's perspective, made possible because we have His Spirit within us lighting up the way with hope. The Psalmist writes,

> *"When I am afraid, I put my trust in you."* Psalms 56:3

When we place our hope in Jesus, we trust Him. It's not that Jesus will ensure we only get good things but that we will get good food. People may say that when good things are happening to them it's a

---

10   See, What a morning! Keith and Kristyn Getty, In Christ Alone, 2007.

sign that God is with them, and it may well be so, but God is always with them no matter what is happening. Things that appear good in a person's life may not be a sign that a person is walking with God. God shows no partiality, so, if a person seems to be getting good things, it is not a sign that God loves them more or that they deserve more. We must not jump to conclusions as there can be alternative explanations. Perhaps the person is walking obediently with God, but perhaps the person is manipulating to get good things. It's equally true that when bad things happen it can be whether we are obedient or whether we are disobedient because we live in a fallen world with fallen people. Jesus made all of this clear.[11] He doesn't ask us to be brave in our own strength. He asks us to trust Him, to know Him, to love Him, to obey Him and to draw upon His grace. Jesus fights to keep us safe. He gives us guidelines by which to dwell in safety. He sends angels. Jesus is our hope. So often, we can be guilty of looking to God to provide someone to fight for us but, in truth, He has done that and so much more through coming in Christ to give His life for us. Job 11:13-18 declares,

"if you would direct your heart right and spread out your hand to Him (God) then you would trust, because there is hope; and you would look around and rest securely."

There are many encouragements in scripture to hope,

"Be strong and take courage all you who hope in the Lord."
Psalm 31:24

"For I hope in you, O Lord." Psalm 38:15

"I recall to mind, therefore I have hope, The Lord's loving kindnesses indeed never cease, for His compassions never fail. They are new

---

11   Luke 13: 1-3, 4-5.

every morning; Great is your faithfulness. The Lord is my portion, says my soul, therefore I have hope in Him. "Lamentations 3:21-24

Throughout the New Testament, we are exhorted to rejoice in hope, to abound in hope through believing, to know the hope of His calling, to remember we are called in one hope. The writer to the Hebrews declares,

"Hope is an anchor of the soul." Hebrews 6:19

"Through hope draw near to God." Hebrews 7:19

John writes in his letter,

"Hope purifies." 1 John 1:3

There are so many references to hope, all demonstrating how important hope is. Living in such hope rejects unbelief and doubt, casts out fear and uncertainty, overcomes despair and depression, and enables us to live in peace and freedom. Living in such hope allows Jesus to be at the centre of our lives and living, and gives Him freedom to work out everything for our good.

As soon as we take our eyes off Jesus and His overall authority and onto the issue that gives us fear, we change the person at the centre of our lives from Jesus to ourselves and we begin to limit our vision as to how we see and understand things, thus allowing fear, doubt and uncertainty to enter in and rob us of peace. We become what we behold.

Jesus is our example. On the road to Gethsemane, He set His eyes to Jerusalem and faced the cross for the joy set before Him. He lived in sure and certain hope, a hope founded on His Father's integrity, and proved by His actions,

"Father, into Your hands, I commit My spirit." Luke 23:46

Jesus is our hope. As we praise and extol Him, our eyes are opened to see Him in power and authority, ruling over everything, and our fearfulness changes to expectancy, our doubting changes to faith, and our unbelief changes to certainty. We know His eye is on the sparrow, and on us. We know that even when we go through the dark shadows that He will walk with us and that we will not be harmed. This hope leads us through the darkness to resurrection joy.

This hope strengthens us through any suffering when we consider the joy set before us. Even in times of doubting Jesus does not forsake us. He didn't abandon Thomas but understood his struggle and revealed the truth to him. In a similar way, Jesus continues to walk with us until we are willing and able to see the truth. Dennis Jernigan, in a song expressing this truth, "You Are My All In All",[12] leads us into worship and renewed confident hope.

Calling up Hope

Now that we know that we have hope as an attribute in our spirits, how can we draw upon this in times of apparent hopelessness? So often our fears, our hurt, our racing thoughts and our stresses cause inner turmoil and make it difficult for us to sense God's presence or to hear His reassurance. But we can choose to focus on Jesus and to ask the Holy Spirit to bring the hope that is in our spirits to the surface. Or we, ourselves, can invite the hope that is within our spirits to come to the surface and show us what he or she is seeing. We can ask the hope in our spirits questions such as, "what is the hope I have?", or "where is God leading me?" We can pray, "spirit hope, shine your light on my path."

---

12   Album: Hands Lifted High: A modern Worship Collection 1998.

One time when I asked my spirit, "what is the hope within me?" I heard the words, "Resurrection Life. Worshipping in the presence of God. Seeing all things accomplished and brought to fulfilment. The rule of God on earth, that I be identified as in Christ, that I pursue my Father. Seeing the angels and archangels worshipping around the throne, seeing our Father God's face of love and seeing Jesus worshipped and adored." Another time, when I asked, "spirit hope what do you see"? I heard, "Outrageous love. As a brand snatched from the fire lest My people forget Me." These words in Zechariah 3:2 and Psalm 59:11 speak of a time when the psalmist was pleading with God to save Israel from their enemies lest it appear that God had left them.

Faith needs hope. Bob Hazlett, while speaking at a conference on "Piercing the Darkness",[13] referred to Hebrews 11:1 with this comment,

> *If faith equals the substance of things hoped for and faith equals the evidence of things not seen, that means things hoped for equals things that are unseen. Without hope we have nothing to attach our faith to. Faith can only bring what is in the unseen realm into the seen realm but if you can't see the unseen realm, you haven't anything to attach your faith to.*

Hope gives revelation from the unseen realm so that faith can bring it into the seen realm. Hope reveals what is and will be, and so needs vision. In Proverbs we are told,

> *"Where there is no vision, the people perish."* Proverbs 29:18a

This gives insight into the importance of hope in our lives as being central to our wellbeing. Doctor Jerome Groopman writes that hope is as strong as any medication he could ever prescribe.[14]

---

13 "Piercing the Darkness", Bethel Church, California.
14 "The Anatomy of Hope. How people prevail in the face of illness" Dr Jerome Groopman MD.

Cancer Wellbeing Centres emphasize that hope is a vital part of healing. We do well to remember that,

"If God be for me who can be against me?" Romans 8:31

When we are infused with supernatural hope in every circumstance of life, we can cope with whatever comes our way. As I was pondering these truths, I sensed the words of a hymn[15] rising from my spirit,

> *Blessed assurance, Jesus is mine*
> *O what a foretaste of glory divine*
> *Heir of salvation, purchase of God*
> *Born of His Spirit, washed in His Blood*
>
> *Perfect submission, all is at rest*
> *I in my Saviour am happy and blessed*
> *Watching and waiting, looking above*
> *Filled with His goodness, lost in His love*
>
> *This is my story, this is my song*
> *Praising my Saviour all the day long*
> *This is my story, this is my song*
> *Praising my Saviour all the day long*

From within our spirits rises hope that is sure and certain and whose core is Jesus.

If our hope is placed on seeing an outcome rather than on Jesus and it doesn't happen, we may begin to lose hope. In this case,

"hope deferred makes the heart grow sick." Proverbs 13:12

---

15   Blessed Assurance, Fanny Crosby and Phoebe P. Knapp 1873.

The Hebrew word for heart in the Old Testament can mean imagination and, as part of us, our imaginations must be set apart for God and continually made holy otherwise they may erode the hope within while we wait. Isaiah has this to say on the subject,

> *"Perfect absolute peace surrounds those whose imaginations are consumed with you; they confidently trust in you."* Isaiah 26:3 TPT

When we are struggling, we can call up the hope that is in our spirits and ask the question, "what do you see?" We then wait patiently for the answer to come so that once again our confidence can be restored. Out of our own experiences we can strengthen others in sure and confident hope.

The hope that is within our spirits is resilient. It is a strength, and when in action can move against any obstructions, persevering no matter what. No matter how often it is crushed or walked over it keeps rising and going on as long as it is encouraged. When we know that God has revealed something to us that is unseen we move forward in sure and certain hope that it is true and will take place. Therefore, vision is imperative to maintaining hope and impairment of vision brings hopelessness. For this reason, it is important to nurture hope with vision and to encourage it in its purpose. We can do this as we spend time in God's presence waiting upon Him,

> *"Those who wait upon the Lord shall renew their strength; they shall mount up with wings like eagles, they shall run and not be weary, they shall walk and not faint."* Isaiah 40:31

Once spirit hope gets encouragement we can move forward again.

Hope is adversely affected by deception and by fear of deception, by accusation through condemnation, and by religious spirits as these undermine truth and vision. Any of these can make this part of our spirits feel despicable, walked over and worthless. If a person looks away from Jesus, the hope within stops being active and the person can feel aimless, as though waiting for action or for excitement but not knowing what. Spirit hope gives and sustains,

"Hope does not disappoint." Romans 5:5

This is the hope mentioned in phrases like, hope for the nations, hope in all circumstances, hope endures. Spirit hope enables us to see the unseen, to see the path with the glorious ending and, along the way, will show us the goodness of the Lord in the land of the living. Spirit hope shows what can be, something lit up which we have yet to walk into and which acts as an impetus to faith,

"For if we hope for what we do not see, we eagerly wait for it with perseverance." Romans 8:25

Recently, after watching a video about someone who had experienced a near death experience in which he had gone to hell, to heaven, and then returned to life, I became scared that I would be going to hell and asked God to show me the truth because if I needed to change something in my life, I wanted to do this. Some days later I had a vision in which I was walking along a narrow path that wound its way through green valleys. As I continued to watch myself walking, I wondered where I was going. Then I saw a signpost, "to the Holy City". I continued walking. As I was passing a group of people who were picnicking and enjoying themselves nearby on the grass, they called me over to join them but I wanted to keep walking and so waved cheerily and continued on my path. Afterwards, as I pondered what I had seen in the vision I realised that God had answered my request by showing me that I was on the road to the Holy City, but at the same time had shown me that I wasn't to be distracted by things that would take me off the path. This vision possibly arose from hope within my spirit as this attribute of the spirit shines the light on the path that we are taking.

What about the wellbeing of others?

Jesus prayed that after his trial Peter would strengthen the brethren. So, also, it is to be that way for us. We can encourage others to open the window of hope in Jesus so that His light comes flooding into their darkness. Through our lives being full of peace and inner strength, we can encourage and strengthen others to look to Jesus in their distress.

Chapter 1.4

Awakening to the Faith of God Within

"It is written: 'I believed; therefore, I have spoken'. Since we have that same spirit of faith, we also believe and therefore speak."
2 Corinthians 4:13

The faith that we have in Christ Jesus, and in His promises to us as His disciples, is a gift of grace from God,

> *"For by grace you have been saved through faith, and that not of yourselves; it is the gift of God, not of works, lest anyone should boast."* Ephesians 2:8

The Holy Spirit draws us into this faith, a faith in Jesus and in all that He offers us through the Cross and resurrection. We are each given, "a measure of faith",

> *"For I say, through the grace given to me, to everyone who is among you, not to think of himself more highly than he ought to think, but to think soberly, as God has dealt to each a measure of faith."* Romans 12:3

This measure of faith releases the life of heaven within us, and begins a work of grace, transforming our minds to come into line with the truth in Christ Jesus as we read, reflect and meditate upon the Word of God, and as we grow in intimacy with our Father God. Faith acts like a mustard seed in that, as we exercise it and have a lifestyle of abiding in Christ, it grows into something large.

> *"Though it is the smallest of all seeds, yet when it grows, it is the largest of garden plants and becomes a tree, so that the birds come and perch in its branches."* Matthew 13:32

Jesus commended the Roman Centurion who had great faith (Matthew 8:9-10), and told His followers,

> *"Truly I tell you, if you have faith as small as a mustard seed, you can say to this mountain, 'Move from here to there,' and it will move. Nothing will be impossible for you."* Matthew 17:20

There will be times when we may waver and doubt in our minds and hearts because they are so easily influenced by others' opinions and by our own fears and anxieties. However, resident within our spirits, is the faith of God,[16] a strong faith, which enables us to focus on Jesus with unwavering confidence and quiet dependency on Him,

> *(Jesus is) One with our Father God, Ancient of Days, through the Spirit who clothes faith with certainty.[17]*

Such calm faith arises within those who walk in humility before the King of Kings and Lord of Lords. It never pushes itself to the forefront but gives us inner deep assurance about the truth revealed in Jesus. Its greatest opponent is pride.

This faith is a gift of God, there from our creation, and having the potential to operate fully once we respond to the sacrificial love of

---

16 Mark 11:22.
17 See, What a morning! Keith and Kristyn Getty, In Christ Alone, 2007

Jesus and our spirits are born again. To some extent, family Christian heritage and the beliefs of the body of believers to which we belong play a part in what we believe. Where our beliefs agree with truth as laid out in scripture then that truth in our minds is in agreement with the truth that is in our spirits. When we grow up in a church culture where divine healing of the body is accepted, our minds have no difficulty in agreeing with our spirits. Our faith in God and in His promises in relation to this are strong. On the other hand, if we are taught beliefs that do not align with a truth of scripture, or if we allow our feelings or experiences to dictate what we believe, then those beliefs in our minds and hearts will conflict with the truth in our spirits. This may lead to a weakening of our ability to move with faith in God and in His promises. For this reason, it is helpful to ask God to show us any unbelief or wrong doctrine that we hold on to because, otherwise, they will hinder us from walking fully in the Spirit. This highlights the importance of reading God's Word while listening to the Holy Spirit, and becoming familiar with all that God teaches us. In some people, this faith within the spirit may be operationally strong from the time of salvation whereas, for others, it may not be allowed full participation due to lack of knowledge.

The grace of faith operates in many ways in our lives. When we respond to the sacrificial love of Jesus, we do so by faith, and are brought into the family of God and assured of eternal life.

As children of God, the Holy Spirit gives us gifts to build up the body of Christ as and when He chooses.[18] One of these is the gift of faith and enables us at a specific time in a specific situation to be a conduit of the power of heaven from God to man.[19]

We also have, resident within us in our spirits, the gift of faith that is an attribute of God. It is the faith of God gifted to us which manifests

---

18   1 Corinthians 12:4-10.
19   A Journey of Discovery by Heather Thompson, 2022, published by Maurice Wylie Media. Section 1.6.

in our lives readily once it is acknowledged and given freedom. We can pray, "open the eyes of our hearts to see the faith that is within us".

We all need to adopt a lifestyle of listening to the voice of the Holy Spirit from within our spirits. Faith in our spirits is the bedrock, the base upon which we are enabled to live by faith,

"The righteous live by faith." Romans 1:17

"Without faith it is impossible to please God." Hebrews 11:6

Jesus said that those who hear God's words and put them into practice, believing God's words, are those who build their lives upon Jesus the Rock, and on faith in Him.[20] Many years ago, a gentleman came regularly to receive prayer for healing from cancer. About two years after he had passed on to be with Jesus, I was visiting a lady who had prayed with him on many occasions. This is what she told me, "After William died Jesus told me that He was very pleased with William because of His strong faith." This strongly contradicts those who reprimand others for lack of faith when it appears that they don't receive the healing for which they are asking. The truth is that we do have faith. We just need to listen to it and,

"walk by faith, not sight." 2 Corinthians 5:7

"looking unto Jesus, the author and finisher of our faith." Hebrews 12:2

We are told that,

"Faith is the substance of things hoped for, the evidence of things not seen." Hebrews 11:1

---

20   Luke 6:47-48.

The Greek word used in this verse, and translated substance, is 'hupostasis'. It speaks of the Divine essence of God giving us a confident assurance in our heart.[21] Substance is not nothing. Rather it is a tangible knowing. When we hear a believer saying, "I know that I know I am saved", they are referring to spiritual substance. They reference two ways of knowing – knowledge in the head, and assurance in the heart. Faith, then, is the ability to believe God with assurance in our mind and heart. It occurs when our hearts are not wavering between two opinions but are totally in agreement with the faith that is an attribute in our spirits.

With increased faith, we believe God more and more, and, consequently, receive more and more from Him.[22]

Faith is faith and we either have faith in God or we do not. I understand the above quotation as meaning that we learn to have faith in God in more areas of our lives through meditating on His Word, receiving revelation and acting upon it. When we move in obedience to God and trust in Him, He confirms His trustworthiness. He gives us confirmations from time to time to encourage our faith.

Faith doesn't have to get. Faith is content in the waiting because faith is in God and in what He has said, not in what we see. This faith that is in our spirits is steady, calm, and has authority. Jesus told His followers,

"Have the faith of God." Mark 11:22

i.e., have the faith that is drawn from God, received from God, imparted by God, established within us by God.

---

21 W.E. Vinee's Expository Dictionary of Old and New Testament Words Vol2 (Old Tappan, NJ :Fleming, H. Revell Company, 1981), 88.

22 Clark, Dennis, Clark Jen, "Releasing the Divine Healer Within".

Through our struggles in life, we come to know God better and, in believing Him we trust Him in more areas. As we draw near to Him, He draws near to us. When we go through something difficult or frightening, through betrayal, misunderstanding or loss, then, as we draw near to Him, He holds us by the hand and walks with us through it. He doesn't offer us ease of life but strength, courage and grace for each moment, all within relationship with Him. As we discover the truth of this, we lean on Him more and more. This is trust. This is faith.

We are commanded to wear the armour of God.[23] As we live in His Word allowing His Word to become part of us, we can speak His Word like a sword. While we draw on His faith within, we cannot be made fearful. When we renew our minds with the mind of Christ through His Word, we cannot be swayed away from thinking in line with Christ. We wear the helmet of salvation, the helmet that protects us from the intrusion of wrong thinking. As we hold everything together in truth, the truth of the word of God, and draw upon this, we will remain strong. As we meditate on the fullness of the Gospel and walk throughout life standing firm on the Good News, we will walk in safety.

Calling up Faith

Faith in our spirits doesn't initiate nor push to the forefront but waits to be invited. Whenever we listen for the voice of faith, we can hear it.

When life circumstances are tough and we are floundering, it can help us to know what we really believe in our spirits. We can listen for the voice of spirit faith when we simply ask the question, "what do I believe?" From within our spirits will come the answer that God

---

23   Ephesians 6:10-17.

knows will strengthen us and reassure us. Sometimes the answer can be a new revelation, something that we didn't know that we believed but which is encouraging. Sometimes it can be humorous, for example, one time when I asked this question my spirit faith said,

"I believe in the weather forecast".

I was puzzled and amused because I knew that this certainly wasn't true for me. When I queried this, God told me that I believe His weather forecast, that when He says that all will be well or, alternatively, that a storm lies ahead, I believe Him. Another time faith within my spirit said,

"I believe in the Holy Grail."

I wasn't sure exactly what this meant and had to gain further insight, but, once I understood, I was pleased. Another time I heard,

"Our God is awesome, powerful, omnipotent."

It is so strengthening to know that such truths are firmly planted within me and not just something I have decided to believe in my head. On another occasion after one of our ministers had been preaching on the man of lawlessness, I asked my spirit faith what I believed and sensed this response,

"I believe that You (Jesus) are able to keep that which I've committed to You until that day." 2 Timothy 1:12

Spirit faith waits to be asked and then looks to God for an answer. This faith doesn't give itself the question in case it is the wrong one. Any questions, statement, scriptures, or encouragements that arise from spirit faith within are initiated by the Holy Spirit.

When we don't know how to pray, calling the faith that is in our spirits will show us what our spirit is receiving and believing from our Father God. Spirit faith is always present but can so easily be ignored when we are focusing on our own thoughts, deductions, emotions and actions, when we rely on ourselves or on others, or when we are apprehensive about the future in some way and fearful of the outcome of circumstances. In such times we may forget to listen to the quiet voice within. When we rely on our human wisdom without seeing with the eyes of faith, we can easily go off track. As we walk in humility depending totally on Jesus and not allowing pride or independence, we can listen to spirit faith speak words which will strengthen us.

We are made with the capacity to believe, and what our heart believes is written on our cells. What we believe is released through faith and communicated to our cells. Believing for healing is not merely asking God to give us something in prayer; it is receiving healing anointing. We can receive healing power from others or directly from the Divine Healer in our own heart. Regardless of what that means, God has created us with the capacity to yield to healing, not just pray for healing. When we open our hearts to the Healer, our cells open their gates to receive Him as well.[24]

The Hebrew word which is often interpreted by the English word, "stripes" in Isaiah 53 can also mean, "fellowship". Intimacy with Jesus releases the faith within to believe the truth that,

"by His stripes we are healed." Isaiah 53:5

Knowing what we believe in our spirits strengthens us against attacks of the enemy. After God had told me that He was giving me the gift of divine health (Book 3) I immediately experienced healing

---

24   Clark Dennis, Jen, "Releasing the Divine Healer Within; The Biology of Belief" Destiny Image, 5 November 2015.

from over thirty years of back pain. There was no doubt about the fact that I was healed. Over the following six months I kept getting pains in different parts of my body but each time I confessed, "I have been given divine health", and they would disappear only to appear somewhere else. Eventually they stopped.

About three months after receiving these words I experienced severe chest pain, breathlessness and heaviness in my chest that was quite debilitating. Again, I declared, "God has given me divine health". Still the discomfort continued and still I declared, "God has given me divine health". I knew with conviction that this was true and there was no doubt in my heart and so I would not let my mind dictate fear or incapacity. One morning several weeks later I awoke with these words rising from my spirit,

"I can do all things through Christ who strengthens me."
Philippians 4:13

Because I recognized them as coming from my spirit, I knew that this was my spirit faith speaking what was in my spirit. My mind and heart were being told, "This is the truth, 'I can do all things through Christ who strengthens me'". Now that my heart (the control centre of my life) was convinced, nothing, not even this debilitating chest thing, was going to stop me in my tracks. I believed deep within that God would enable me. At this time, I didn't need to work at bringing every thought captive in obedience to the scripture. Because I had revelation from my spirit which, in turn, had convinced my heart, my mind was instructed in the truth and random thoughts went silent in the face of my declaration. This confidence remained with me throughout the month that the discomfort continued, and I have been free of it since. Hearing these words from spirit faith greatly encouraged me because it confirmed to me that I really believed deep within with all my being that I could do all things through Christ who strengthens me. Spirit faith had revealed the strength of the faith within me. Such faith produces works, the fruit of faith being seen in a person's life. Declaring what we believe silences contrary thoughts. Faith and our words work together.

Important Footnote

Presumption is not faith at all. Either, God will give us revelation to shed light on the path that we are to take so that we can move in obedience to the revelation with the faith we have, or God will release the gift of faith in a situation, without us needing the understanding, so that we can move in response to that faith. Listening to our spirits and to spirit faith is important if we are going to walk in the spirit. As we release our desire, our faith to Him, He releases His grace.

Spirit faith runs the race, enabling us to keep on believing despite what we see, hear, or feel with the natural senses. All glory be to God!

Chapter 1.5

Awakening to the Revelation of God Within

"However, as it is written: 'What no eye has seen, what no ear has heard, and what no human mind has conceived' – the things God has prepared for those who love him – these are the things God has revealed to us by his Spirit. The Spirit searches all things, even the deep things of God."

1 Corinthians 2:9-10

Another of the attributes of our Father God, which is resident within our spirits, is the ability to move with revelation given by the Spirit of God. This can be at God's instigation or through our requesting it. Revelation is seeing things through God's eyes. It is the revealing of things and is for the "now". The Spirit of God gives us revelation so that we understand the secrets and mysteries of the Kingdom of God. He reveals the heart of our Father God and tells us what Jesus wants us to know. He tells us of things yet to come. He glorifies Jesus.[25] Through revelation from within our spirits we see with our spiritual eyes, hear with our spiritual ears and our hearts are opened to understand spiritual truth.

---

25   John 16:8-15.

The Holy Spirit will only reveal what God wants us to know. Through revelation we are given fresh insight, an alertness to something that we haven't taken under our notice or a fuller understanding of what we have already perceived. We may be given understanding that helps us to resolve issues. Generally, in life, our own inadequacies and inferiorities can blind us to the true picture and maybe there are times when we only see what we want to see. Since revelation in our spirits is a part of us that is tuned into the revelation of God, when we look through the eyes of spirit revelation we will be enabled to see into the spiritual realm and see things that we cannot see physically. We see through the eyes of God and are given God's perspective on what seems apparently without hope in the world. Importantly, we see others through His eyes.

We will receive revelation from God if we are willing to see without prejudice. However, if we have a pre-conceived notion or desire as to what we would really like to be shown in response to a query, we cannot be sure that what we see will be coming to us from God. Before asking for revelation, we need to wait in God's presence laying down our own desires until we know that we are willing to see or hear whatever God chooses to show or tell us.

There is a close link between revelation and knowledge as revelation brings knowledge and, with it, understanding. For example, in Mark 2:8 we read that Jesus knew in His spirit what they were thinking. Some manuscripts use the word "see". Through seeing, He knew and was given understanding about what the onlookers were thinking. We can pray prayers like, "Lord, please forgive me for not seeking your revelation, and restore my ability to see life through your eyes. May faith rise within me and may I worship You with all my heart, mind and spirit. Amen."

An open vision in which God spoke to me about the gift of revelation within

One morning in May 2003 God asked me the question, "What are you going to be doing to-day?" I waited for a moment and found an answer forming from my spirit. I replied, "Setting about setting free the captives". Even as I was answering I was thinking, "What does that mean? Is it different from what I do in the deep ministry that I am involved in as in this ministry I am frequently in a position to free captives in the name of Jesus? Somehow, I felt that God was showing me a different kind of freeing the captives.

As I pondered this, I saw a child sleeping and when she awoke, she could not open her eyes. I found myself saying, "ephphatha" at which the child slowly did open them. She was gentle, quiet and thoughtful. She asked me, "What name has been given you?" From within my spirit came the answer, "Mother of many". God had called me by this name because I have been a mother to many fragmented child parts in ministry. "And what name has been given to you?" I asked. "Keeper of the key", she replied. "The key to what?" I asked. "The key to where the captives are. This is the age of revelation."

In the spirit I could see this child reach out to me with the key in her hand and so I took it. I couldn't think what to do with it other than hand it in the spirit to Jesus. He then gave me to understand that He was using the key to unlock the gate and set the "children of revelation" free. This is an example of one of the many ways in which God illustrates a truth to enable understanding. In this case He was personifying the spirit attribute of revelation. He then invited me to call my spirit revelation back. I understood that in some way He was restoring the fullness of the spirit attribute of revelation in me. I did this and then prayed that she (my child of revelation) would become an integral part of me.

These "children of revelation" are "children" of worship and dedication to God, inwardly strong and fearless, having been through everything that prepares them for the type of persecution they may face. I found myself singing a new song of worship with the theme, "Glorify the King". It came so readily without effort, and confirmed to me what I believe I had witnessed. I was told to write down the revelation and reminded that God had told me on several occasions that "my tongue was the tongue of a ready writer". I was told, "These are the days of Joel."

The child told me that there had been many who had tried to get the key to use it themselves and bring on revival. She also told me that she had recognized the word, "ephphatha", and knew that she was to give the key to me and that I would give it to Jesus. Only now did I realize the significance of the word, "ephphatha" as it was a word used by Jesus to open the ears and release the tongue of a man who was deaf and dumb.[26] Now God had used it to open the eyes of revelation. I also got the impression of the Church rising out of the ashes.

In choosing to go our own way and wanting knowledge for ourselves we reject the revelation that God wants to give us through the Holy Spirit within. But God, in His mercy, has kept the ability to receive revelation in our spirits safe for us. When anyone repents of rejecting knowledge from God and asks God to restore it God will do just that. This means that at any time we can call upon the revelation from within our spirits for insight and understanding.

How does the gift of revelation that is resident within help us?

The gift of revelation that is resident within strengthens and encourages us through the spiritual revealing of insights accompanied

---

26   Mark 7:31-37.

by truth. One day, as I was walking along the shore, I saw a small fish floundering on the beach. I picked it up and threw it into the water but as I watched it was swept back onto land. I picked it up once again and heaved it with all my strength into the depths of the sea. This time it was not beached by the waves. As I walked on, I pondered the lesson emerging. Only when I plunge deeply into the living waters of the Spirit of God will I remain safely in His love. I was being reminded of the blessing, the benefit, the life, joy and the freedom that comes from plunging into the oceans of God's love and I was being encouraged by the fact that God had chosen to speak to me by revealing spiritual truth using ordinary everyday things. This is seeing the unfamiliar in the familiar. God encourages us to "look behind" what we see with our physical eyes so that we walk in tune with the Spirit of God.

This revelation resident within us helps us to see what God wants to show us, whether it be personal, or for the Church, our country or the world. An encouraging personal example occurred when my spirit revelation stated that I was about my Father's business. On occasion, I have had revelation from God about something that is adversely affecting a country and so have been enabled to know how to pray specifically. Later I have been encouraged by the outcome. Jesus taught about revelation,

> *"Life does not come only from eating bread but from God. Life flows from every revelation from his mouth."* Luke 4:4 TPT

and then exemplified it when feeding the five thousand,

> *"... Jesus took the five loaves and two fish, gazed into heaven, and gave thanks to God. He broke the bread and the two fish and distributed them to his disciples to serve the people - and the food was multiplied in front of their eyes!"* Mark 6:41 TPT

In this account we are told that Jesus shifted His focus from the limited amount of food offered and, while thanking God for it, "gazed into heaven" looking towards God. Was God revealing to Him that He would multiply the food until there was more than enough? Such an insight given through revelation releases faith.

Calling up Revelation

Revelation from within helps us to see in the spiritual why something is happening in the natural. So often we think we are looking and observing but at times we may not be seeing as we could and should and, consequently, we fail to act. There are many occasions when we don't know or understand what is going on and how we are to pray. Spirit revelation can help us to see what God wants us to know and understand about the source of a problem. Whenever we are finding it difficult to understand something, we can call upon spirit revelation to show what God is revealing e.g., if I am perplexed as to why someone is having difficulty with nightmares, I can ask God to reveal the cause to me through the revelation part of my spirit. As I call upon revelation within to rise up and show me what she is seeing I am calling to the forefront my spirit ability to see what God wants to show me. Then I can act upon the information or question God further. We read in scripture that Abraham asked God questions when he didn't understand. Mary, when told she would have a baby, asked the angel,

"How can this be, since I do not know a man?" Luke 1:34 NKJV

In scripture, asking questions didn't mean that people didn't have faith but that they were trying to understand. God answers such questions. Answers may help us to believe and move with faith. For example, if we want to see God heal mental illness then we need to be willing to spend time with Him seeking Him about it through asking questions and feeding our minds with His words, and perhaps recalling testimonies to encourage faith. Revelation gives understanding and can be a precursor to our being able to exercise faith in a specific situation.

Once this gift of revelation was returned in fullness, we found we were more alert to discerning deceptions and praying appropriately. In one ministry session, a client was struggling with the feeling that he wasn't close to Jesus despite the fact that his words indicated that he was exercising total commitment. As we talked, the revelation from within our spirits enabled us to see symptoms that threw light on his problem. His commitment was legalistic, his thoughts chaotic, and he aggressively refuted anything I said. Depending on the focus, this client was totally committed to Jesus, to people, to anything. Clearly a religious spirit was strongly influencing him. As a result, this client was greatly deprived of hope, life, faith and love and was functioning on a spirituality of do and do not. As we explored further, we learnt that he had attended a spiritualist church and had entered into some strange practices prior to coming to faith in Jesus, and so was now being affected by the presence of a religious spirit while mistaking it for the Holy Spirit. Once all this was resolved, this person could commit to Jesus very deeply and worshipfully and enjoy a relationship and commitment without the former driven-ness.

Spirit revelation shows us that God is with us. It removes fear and gives us confidence and security. Just as there are difficulties for someone physically blind so, also, we can be in danger if we don't see spiritually. Seeing spiritually can comfort us and, when needed, warn us.

Examples from Scripture showing revelation at work

- The people wept when Ezra read the book of the law – the Spirit and the Word working together to give revelation. (Nehemiah 8:9)

- Ezekiel was taken by the Spirit to Jerusalem to see what was happening there. (Ezekiel 8:3)

- Simeon had a revelation of Jesus as the consolation of Israel. (Luke 2:25-32)

- Zacharias, Mary and Joseph all saw angels. (Luke 1:11-17; 26-38, Matthew 1:18-21; 2:13-14)

- The patriarch, Joseph, was given dreams and interpretation. (Genesis 37:1-44:9)

- Noah was told that mankind was to be wiped out except for Noah, his family and designated animals. (Genesis 6:9-7:5)

- Those looking on into the fiery furnace saw a fourth man. (Daniel 3:8-30)

- Peter was given fresh revelation accompanied by understanding while in a trance in which he saw a sheet with all kinds of animals being let down to the earth and heard God speak. (Acts 10:9-47)

- Samuel was given revelation by God that Eli's family sin would not be atoned for by sacrifices or offerings. (1 Samuel 3:1-21)

- John the apostle was given revelation of what was to come. (Book of Revelation)

- Isaiah was given a revelation of the Lord enthroned on high and with His train filling the temple. (Isaiah 6:1-10)

- The prophets were given revelation for the nations. e.g., (Acts 16:6-10)

- Peter, James and John saw Jesus transfigured and "knew" that Moses and Elijah were standing on either side of Jesus. (Matthew 17:1-5)

- When Jesus asked the disciples, *"Whom do men say that I am?"*, Peter replied *"You are the Christ, the Son of the Living God"*. (Mark 8:27-29)

- The two walking on the road to Emmaus experienced burning in their hearts as they listened to Jesus expound the scriptures. (Luke 24:13-35)

- On the shore after the resurrection John recognised Jesus. (John 21:1-9)

- Elisha "saw" the chariot and horses of fire. (2 Kings 2:1-12)

- Elisha prayed that God would open his servant's eyes to receive revelation. (2 Kings 6:17)

Prayer and dependency on God are keys for Spirit-to-spirit revelation. What we see through revelation to our spirits becomes a certainty to us. Along with seeing through spirit revelation there comes a conviction of the truth revealed, and a knowing or understanding as to what it means. Unlike a truth that is held in the mind and can be influenced by others or by our own wavering opinions, and unlike a truth held in the heart that can be influenced by our feelings, a truth held in the spirit is firmly rooted and established. Once we become aware of such truth and confess it, our hearts stop wavering and we are enabled to stand firm and to keep going, no matter what assails our minds or emotions. Revelation has power. We are limited in how much we see and understand through our physical sight but when we see as Jesus sees, we can have greater understanding, wisdom, peace and generosity of heart, and the outcome is more likely to be peaceable. Above all, with the eyes of revelation we see Jesus. As we desire to see with our spirits so we will. It is like having a blindfold or a veil removed so that we see farther in all dimensions and directions.

Jesus lived the whole of His life with full revelation. When He looked upon Jerusalem and wept, He was seeing more than buildings and people walking about. He was seeing their true spiritual state, their blindness to Him, their rejection of Him and the painful consequences for them. When He looked at the Samaritan woman at the well, He saw that she had had five husbands and that her present companion was not married to her. He saw a woman who was thirsty for His living water and who would drink from it and become an evangelist. Seeing her thirst He shared truth with her, which in turn led to many seeking Him.

Some of the reasons why revelation can strengthen us

- So that we know how to pray. In Daniel 9 we read that it was revealed to Daniel that the time had come for the fulfilment of what he had read about in Jeremiah 27. What was he to do? He was to use this knowledge to pray. During World War Two, on several occasions, while in prayer God gave Rees Howells revelation as to how to pray. History has recorded that each of the revelations given to Rees for prayer were instrumental in stopping some aspect of Hitler's advance.

- So that we are reassured. For example, while at sea during a storm, Paul was able to reassure everyone that, although the ship would be lost, they would all be saved. In that same revelation, Paul was told that he must stand trial before Caesar in Acts 27:13-26.

- To enable generosity of heart through having greater understanding of what is affecting another. Examples are Jesus with the Samaritan woman found in John 4:1-26 and with Zacchaeus in Luke 19:1-10.

- To prepare us through forewarning so as to give us strengthening and encouragement before crisis. An example of this was one morning as I awoke, I saw myself in a small boat on a stormy sea. While I watched myself being tossed about, a scripture reference came to mind from Psalm 124. An hour later a friend phoned to say that God had impressed upon her that Psalm 124 had a message for me. Having read it I continued with my work. Later, I came under strong verbal attack and returned home totally undermined. I sank into a chair and called out, "Please give me something to read, Lord!" Back came a gentle reply, "I already have". Psalm 124 gave me the much-needed comfort of knowing that God had shown me that He had known what would happen. Many examples of forewarning are found in scripture, for example, Joseph being warned in a dream to flee to Egypt. Matthew 2:13-14.

- To teach us or give insight. For example, through a vision, Cornelius was instructed to send for Peter and through a trance Peter was taught that the gospel was for Gentiles as well as Jews as told in Acts 10. Paul had revelation that his imprisonment would lead to the spreading of the gospel and so was strengthened to bear the confinement. Philippians 1:14

- To reveal some aspect of God's plan in our lives, maybe for encouragement. The Holy Spirit had revealed to Simeon that he would see the Lord's Christ before he would die. Luke 2:25-32

- To guide us and convince us of the right path. Simeon was moved by the Spirit to be in the right place at the right time and so see the Lord's Christ. The wise men saw a specific star among many which they believed would lead them to the Messiah. Matthew 2:1-2

- To help us see what all along has been there but has not been taken under our notice e.g., Elisha's servant. 2 Kings 6:17

- To give us understanding. For example, we may suddenly see how an ability can be used in a creative way to enhance a service. We may see a gracious quality in another and be able to encourage that person by sharing the knowledge with them.

- To help others. We may see a specific gifting in someone and so be able to encourage them in developing this. We may see fear or loneliness in a person and, through further revelation, encourage and know how to pray for them.

The most profound revelation of all is that of the sin-bearing of Christ Jesus. We can know it cerebrally, but when we grasp it by revelation in our spirits it changes the head knowledge into a deeply held conviction.

When I asked God to explain to me the differences between the hope, faith and revelation that is resident within us as Christians this was His response,

> *Hope reveals what is true and certain to come in Jesus Christ. Faith believes what is true but cannot be seen (hope can be instrumental in the assurance of faith). Revelation is the seeing of all things great and small, the concerns of God for His world and His people. It reveals the detail for the now, that which God is showing for the now and which is true in the now.*

On our life's journey, we can call upon this gift of revelation at any time. It enables us to see in the spirit what we may not otherwise see, perhaps seeing in the spirit what is behind that which can be seen naturally and giving us a more complete understanding. Revelation from God gives us knowledge which in turn strengthens us and encourages us on our journey.

Let us see our life journey through the eyes of Jesus with faith and revelation. Let us no longer walk in 2D, using mind and heart and relying only on our physical senses, but walk in 3D, using mind, heart and spirit, relying on God to give us His perspective and to see life experiences through His eyes. Let us be a peculiar people, who by the grace of God, can celebrate in the face of difficulties and experience joy when the going gets tough, all because we have intimacy and companionship with our Heavenly Father and see life through His eyes.

Above all, let us ask for further revelation about our Father's love for us and about Jesus as the Son of Righteousness, King of Glory, Prince of Peace, Lord of Heaven and Earth so that we may celebrate His gift of love and life to us.

Chapter 1.6

Awakening to the Life of God Within

"But if Christ is in you, then even though your body is subject to death because of sin, the Spirit gives life because of righteousness."
Romans 8:10

The life that is resident in our spirits thrives as we worship God in spirit and truth with hearts full of wonder and love towards God.[27] Such worship is lived out through looking to and trusting Jesus,[28] and through reaching out to others with God's love, caring for the lost, the lonely and the afflicted. It is a lifestyle of worship lived out in holiness.[29] Any superficial participation in worship on our part quenches this life within and any atmosphere that denies the Lordship of Jesus can smother it. This life in our spirits is affected adversely by darkness, death, religiosity, false worship or worldliness in the Church. It seeks the true Church.

We can ask God to restore or release this life in our spirits to all its fullness within us. Knowing that we are His children, welcomed, loved and wanted, we can relate to Him spontaneously, trusting and totally dependent on Him. When God restores life in all its

---

27 Psalm 86:12, John 4:24.
28 Proverbs 3:5.
29 James 1:27.

fullness, we experience a difference, greater freedom in worship, greater abundance of life, life that bubbles with joy even in the face of difficulties. It is life with a capital 'L' that flows like a river from our spirits bringing freedom and joy wherever it goes. As God's child, we enjoy life with exuberance, seeing it through the eyes of wonder, revelation and faith. This is the overflow of the abundant life that Jesus promises to those who trust Him.[30]

This aspect of our spirit is gentle and emanates the light of Christ,

> *"In Him was life and that life was the light of men. The light shines in the darkness but the darkness has not overcome."* John 1:4-5

> *"You are the light of the world. A city on a hill cannot be hidden. Neither do people light a lamp and put it under a bowl. Instead, they put it on a stand, and it gives light to everyone in the house. In the same way let your light so shine before men, that they may see your good deeds and praise your Father in Heaven."* Matthew 5:14-16

Nowhere is the light of Jesus seen more clearly than in the countenance of a person who has a lifestyle of worshipping God. Jesus told the religious leaders of the day,

> *"You study the scriptures diligently because you think that in them you have eternal life. These are the very scriptures that testify about me, yet you refuse to come to Me to have life."* John 5:39-40

Once we have eyes to see, we become more aware of just how many times throughout scripture we are told that God wants to fellowship with each one of us.

The presence of feelings that suddenly appear such as intolerance or frustration, misery, lostness or dullness may be evidence that

---

30   John 10:10.

something is not quite right with this life within our spirits. It is the aspect of our spirits that gets most affected by death and darkness. Sometimes it can be that spirit life is disillusioned with the way life appears if it doesn't seem to be much different from life in the darkness. It can be that this spiritually hungry part is missing the reality of true worship. For example, if people are chatting during a service of worship this life in our spirits may be distracted from focussing on their heart's desire to worship. When we sense unease, we can ask God for insight and, once we understand the cause and make an appropriate response, the disturbing feeling will leave.

When we meditate on the love that God the Father has for us this life within springs into worship. When we join with others in worship and listen attentively to Spirit-inspired teaching once again the life in our spirits responds. This aspect of our spirit expects God to do mighty things but needs to be nurtured through worship and God's Word. It is tender, like a crop swaying in the wind which even during a storm will bend rather than break, although the potential for breaking is there. Like light, life doesn't fight for its place but quietly shines through the darkness. Being actively alert to this amazing attribute from God within us enables us to connect at a wider and deeper level with Him than previously. Let us enjoy this fullness of life.

Chapter 1.7

Awakening to the
Wisdom of God Within

---

*"This is what we speak, not in words taught us by human wisdom
but in words taught by the Spirit, explaining spiritual realities with
Spirit-taught words."*
1 Corinthians 2:13

Throughout scripture we are urged to seek the wisdom of God,

*"If any of you lacks wisdom, you should ask God, who gives
generously to all without finding fault, and it will be given to
you."* James 1:5

*"Get wisdom, get understanding; do not forget my words or turn
away from them. Do not forsake wisdom, and she will protect you;
love her, and she will watch over you. The beginning of wisdom is
this: Get wisdom. Though it cost all you have, get understanding.
Cherish her, and she will exalt you; embrace her, and she will
honour you."* Proverbs 4:5-8

*"for the foolishness of God is wiser than human wisdom, and the
weakness of God is stronger than human strength."* 1 Corinthians 1:25

We also learn from scripture how important God's wisdom is in our spheres of influence and when we are being challenged,

"See, I have chosen Bezalel son of Uri, the son of Hur, of the tribe of Judah, and I have filled him with the Spirit of God, with wisdom, with understanding, with knowledge and with all kinds of skills." Exodus 31:2-3

"Now Joshua son of Nun was filled with the spirit of wisdom because Moses had laid his hands on him. So, the Israelites listened to him and did what the Lord had commanded Moses." Deuteronomy 34:9

"So, give your servant a discerning heart to govern your people and to distinguish between right and wrong. For who is able to govern this great people of yours?" 1 Kings 3:9

"But when they arrest you, do not worry about what to say or how to say it. At that time, you will be given what to say." Matthew 10:19

"For I will give you words and wisdom that none of your adversaries will be able to resist or contradict." Luke 21:15

What is the wisdom of God?

"But the wisdom that comes from heaven is first of all pure, then peace loving, considerate, submissive, full of mercy and good fruit, impartial and sincere. Peacemakers who sow in peace raise a harvest of righteousness." James 3:17-18

How can we discern between what is earthly wisdom and what is Godly wisdom?

> *"Who is wise and understanding among you? Let him show by good conduct that his works are done in the meekness of wisdom. But if you have bitter envy and self-seeking in your hearts, do not boast and lie against the truth. This wisdom does not descend from above, but is earthly, sensual, demonic. For where envy and selfish seeking exist, confusion and every evil thing will be there."* James 3:13-16

Wisdom is part of our Godly inheritance, lost to some extent through inherited iniquity and our own sinfulness. If our hearts are in any way not pure, not peace loving or considerate, not submissive nor full of mercy, or are not impartial or sincere, then we are unable to receive the wisdom of God. He invites us to ask Him for wisdom and He promises to give it to anyone who asks but if our heart attitudes are not righteous then we are unable to receive His gift.

How can our heart attitudes be changed to be like those of Jesus? First of all, we must want to change so as to be like Him in character. Then, as we study His Word, listening to revelation from the Holy Spirit and responding, we will be made clean.[31] Whenever we become convicted of, and turn deliberately away from, an ungodly thought or act we are being purified and as a consequence can receive God's wisdom and bring forth peace.

One day, while praying, I found myself being led by the Spirit into repenting of prejudices that I hadn't been aware of. The words were flowing out from my spirit as truth and I sensed that the potential to move in any of them was inherent in my fallen nature. As I finished, I saw myself climbing a fence stile to sit with others and then I heard a gentle voice say, "now you have wisdom". As I puzzled over this,

---

31   John 15:3, 1 Corinthians 2:13.

the passage on wisdom in James 3 came to mind. This scripture encapsulated much of what God had been drawing my attention to. He was revealing to me that prejudices act like a cover over the wisdom that is resident in our spirits, and that it is only as we turn away from such prejudices that the wisdom in our spirits is set free. As we read earlier, James tells us that this wisdom from above is impartial, signalling that we are not to be bigoted or to show favouritism.[32] In 1 Corinthians 3 Paul points out that sectarianism is carnal, that where there is division, envy and strife we are behaving with prejudice and are not walking in the Spirit. We can be guilty of showing prejudice, against the poor versus the rich, against those who in some ways are different from us, whether in education, class, personality, religious affiliation, lifestyle or culture. We can make judgements based on our preferences and, through our assumptions, discriminate. We can show prejudice against ourselves. Fear can drive us to wrong understanding and conclusions which in turn lead to words that are harmful. Jesus consistently demonstrated a right spirit and good motives and, even when He used some pretty strong, divisive statements in confronting the Sadducees and Pharisees, He wasn't doing it from prejudice but from a heart that called out for righteousness. Peacemakers need the wisdom of God, and to receive the wisdom of God we need to be peacemakers and without prejudice.

Sometimes we can confuse pacifism with peace-making. A pacifist may opt for a peace that is superficial and that doesn't address the issue. Anyone who has been controlled in life by fear may learn to seek peace in this way and, indeed, may even allow others to walk over them in order to restore peace. Such behaviour is merely a protective mechanism and allows others to have their own way, even when it is unjust.

---

32   James 3:17-18; James 3:13-16.

God creates us to be peacemakers, children of God who will see God.[33] A peacemaker aims for true, deep lasting peace, even at cost to themselves. They draw others together, enabling all involved to seek revelation and understanding, and to come to agreement through the truth. Wisdom is given as we seek God's face and so is a choice. We can ask God to restore to us our Godly inheritance of wisdom, and then grow in His wisdom by sowing the Word of God into our lives so that our hearts are righteous places within which it can flourish. When a person is submissive to God and has Godly motives such as sincerity, consideration and mercy towards others then, in their desire to help and affirm them, they will be given wisdom to do so as they seek God's help. Through revelation, they will be enabled to see what is going on behind the masks of self-protection and thereby be compassionate. In yearning to be a peacemaker, that part of our spirit that has wisdom can bring the fruit of wisdom to alleviate emotional distress and hidden pain. When we honour one another, we discern the good that is within and so can encourage each other into full potential in Christ.

Wisdom from God is creative. When we walk in the wisdom of God, we receive understanding for ourselves and for others. We can give Godly impartation of wisdom into any sphere of society thus causing people to take note and recognise the wisdom as coming from God. Godly wisdom will provide solutions far beyond our natural wisdom or experience, an invisible dimension of God-given ideas,

> *"the treasures of darkness and hidden riches in the secret places."*
> Isaiah 45:3

> *"the revealing of mysteries."* Daniel 2:28

---

33   Matthew 5:9.

A number of years ago, I heard a remarkable story of how God had given a salesman some much needed practical wisdom for his business. This man recounted how he had owned a business which sold car parts for repairs and that they used a computer program for ordering and invoicing these spare parts. As the business grew, the computer program became inadequate. He didn't want the expense of buying a different one and so tried to find someone who could adapt the one they had. After some unsuccessful attempts he contacted the person who had written the program but he wasn't willing to help.

Throughout this time, he prayed and continued praying asking God for a solution. One night in a dream he saw a series of analytical steps which he then jotted down even though he couldn't understand them. Thinking it might be an insight for adjusting the program, he woke his wife who was more computer literate than he and insisted they go to the office at that very moment. Using the information given in the dream she was able to adapt the program thus saving them a great deal of money. It is truly wonderful to experience God's help in our everyday lives.

Solomon was invited by God to ask for whatever he wanted God to do for him. In response Solomon said,

> *"Give me wisdom and knowledge, that I may lead this people,*
> *for who is able to govern this great people of yours?"*
> 2 Chronicles 1:10

One translation of the Hebrew suggests that he asked for a hearing ear. A hearing ear gives us access to God's wisdom. Psalm 131:1 (NLT) records David as saying,

> *"I do not concern myself with matters too great or too awesome for*
> *me to grasp!"*

Jesus tells us to seek first His Kingdom and everything else will be added. We are told that the poor in spirit,

> *"are blessed for theirs is the kingdom of heaven."* Matthew 5:3

As we live dependent on God to give us all we need we will be given knowledge and wisdom for our daily living.

In conclusion, we recall that Paul gives us a focus as to why the wisdom of God is essential to the church,

> *"His intent was that now, through the church, the manifold wisdom of God should be made known to the rulers and authorities in the heavenly realms."* Ephesians 3:10

Chapter 1:8
Awakening to Companionship with God

"We proclaim to you what we have seen and heard so that you also may have fellowship with us. And our fellowship is with our Father God and with his Son, Jesus Christ."
1 John 1:3

Another example of God using personification to give me understanding was when He taught me about the ability that we have in our spirits to have full companionship with Him. One morning, I was shown a baby who was still in the womb. As the vision continued, she grew up to three years old. I heard the word, "behold", used repeatedly with reference to her eyes, her ears and her mouth. It was clear to me that this child was aware that she was being held by God and knew Him as her Father but that she had become covered, although not influenced, by the evil inheritance of wickedness. She was hidden away in the depths, as though buried, but still in her Father God's arms.

My response was not one of excited anticipation, but of a sense of hopelessness, weariness and despair. I felt as though I was battle weary and didn't have the energy to do anything about it. The child encouraged me to ask God to remove the veil from over my eyes and ears and mouth so that I could behold our Father God, her companion. I did so but continued to feel the overwhelming misery within. Then she asked me to lift high the bowl of suffering and offer it to God so that He might take it away. Following the leading of the Holy Spirit, I offered up my bowl of suffering to our Father God and gave Him all the evil and the wickedness in my heart. Then I asked Him to give me His inheritance for me. I felt calm and peaceful, drawn into a place of rest. I heard the words, *"Who will ascend the hill?"* followed by the response, *"He who has clean hands and a pure heart."* Psalm 24:3-4.

Repentance from our own sin, receiving forgiveness and cleansing brings us into a place of reconciliation with God. Release from the consequences of generational evil and wickedness frees us into being able to enjoy greater fullness of companionship with God our Father, seeing God's glory.

This deeply ingrained evil and wickedness is referred to in Jeremiah where God says through the prophet,

> *"the heart is deceitful above all things, and desperately wicked; who can know it?"* Jeremiah 17:9

God is saying that we cannot know the full potential for evil that is within each of us and so He invites us to pray prayers like,

> *"Search me, O God, and know my heart; try me and know my anxieties; and see if there is any wicked way in me, and lead me in the way everlasting."* Psalm 139:24

Such a prayer invites God to bring sinful thoughts, attitudes and actions to our attention. We know of many times when He has led us to repent of sinful thoughts, attitudes and actions that we are aware of having committed but He may lead us to repent of things we know we have never done and never thought of doing. Why should we repent of these? Repenting is simply a decision to turn away from sin towards Him and journey through life with Him. Asking God to remove inherited iniquity frees us from the potential to be influenced by such iniquity. Jesus said that murder begins as hatred in the heart.[34] Iniquity which originates in the heart can often lead to sinful action and consequent loss of companionship with our Father God.

The Church is a living body and so we may ask ourselves the question as to whether she is being adversely influenced by past iniquity. Is the Church struggling because she does not understand the battle waging for her soul? Turning to God and confessing our hidden fleshly desires, asking Him to lead us out into freedom will free us (the Church) to live from her spirit and rejoice in ever-deepening fellowship with Him.

Restoration to greater fullness of this attribute enables us to grow in our enjoyment of companionship with God and to experience our Father's love and acceptance of us and His desire to be close to us. It is the seventh restoration of the attributes of God that exist within our reborn spirits: love, hope, faith, life, revelation, wisdom and companionship.

Blessings that arise from these gifts of grace which have been imparted to us

Being awakened to and consistently aware of the inner strength that is available to us from within our spirits enables us to stand firm during difficult times. Even though our emotions may fluctuate and be distressed and our minds tormented, our spirits remain steady, secure and calm, and we are enabled to trust that God will see us

---

34 Matthew 5:21.

through. Many have witnessed to this truth throughout long periods of illness or heartbreak.

Alertness to what we can see and believe from our spirits influences our heart beliefs, removes doubt and double-mindedness and enables us to become deeply rooted and established in the love of God our Father. Our gratitude to Jesus as our Saviour and Lord increases and we become more reliant upon the Holy Spirit as our teacher and guide.

All spirit attributes walk the way of the Cross with hope leading the way. All are redemptive. God showed us that we can think of the attributes as travelling in formation in the shape of a cross as this helps us to understand how they work together. They travel the way of the Cross, the way of communion with our Father God. They are one. They are gifts of grace, attributes of God Himself.

Hope
strong & quiet,
sees the way and
knows where it is
going, needs vision

Love
a force,
exuberant

Life
worships,
gentle, emanates
light, adversely
affected by religion

Faith
quiet, confident
adversely
affected by pride

Reveilation
quiet, observant,
lights up the way so
that we can see
and discern danger

Wisdom
calm, creative,
impartial, listens,
gives
understanding

Companionship
knows our Father
God, enjoys His
presence and
beholds His glory

If one of the attributes in our spirits is adversely affected and stops moving forward, then all stop until that one is restored. Because Hope sees the way and knows where it is going it leads. It is quiet but strong and waits patiently if any of the others hesitate. Love and Faith are the two arms of the Cross with Life central. Love is exuberant and full of fun whereas Life and Faith are quiet and steady. Revelation reflects and observes, taking up the rear guard behind Hope, Life, Love and Faith. It shines like a torch, lighting up the path ahead so that the others can see and the person discern danger. Behind revelation come wisdom and companionship supporting and enabling the others. They are one, the Spirit of God in our spirits.

All seven attributes enable us to see in the unseen realm and receive from that realm. They enable us to live from heaven towards earth and thus to bring in fulfilment of the phrase, "Thy kingdom come, Thy will be done on earth as in heaven".

Sometimes God will cause them to come to the fore with a message from Him or so as to reveal some truth that we believe in the core of our being but may be overlooking. We can call upon any of the attributes in our spirits at any time to help us in our walk with God:

- Calling up hope reveals what is to come, gives vision, and counters despair and hopelessness.

- Calling up faith counters doubts and fears and strengthens us in our faith. It reveals what we believe.

- Calling up life leads us to worship and worshipping brings more of life to the surface and leads us into fuller revelation of the love of God for us.

- Calling up love reveals the heart of our Father God towards us and others and helps us to love those we find difficult to love. Frequently God initiates this.

- Calling up revelation gives insight, understanding, knowledge and direction in the present.

- Calling up wisdom reveals what to say or do in a difficult situation. Wisdom brings resolution.

- Calling up companionship invites companionship with God, the revealing of our Father God's love and acceptance of us and of His desire to be close,

"But he who unites himself with the Lord is one with Him in spirit." 1 Corinthians 6: 17

I offer the following as a prayer,

Our Lord Jesus prayed for you, that you may be one as our Father God was in Him and He is in you. Be blessed, for the Lord Jesus has given you the glory that Father God gave Him, so that you may be one as they are one.[35] I bless you with uniting yourself with the Lord Jesus, with being one with Him in spirit and being a life-giving spirit to all you meet. I bless you with spiritual fervour, that you may speak and teach accurately the things of the Lord and be diligent and enthusiastic in serving Him, being one with Him and devoted to Him in spirit, soul and body[36] ... I bless you to be able to differentiate between the thoughts of your spirit and the attitudes of your soul. I bless you with being able to relate to others spirit to spirit. I bless you with responding to situations and circumstances from the depths of your spirit, not from your soul. I bless you with being humble, contrite and repentant, so that you will be revived and renewed in heart and spirit by the Holy One who inhabits eternity.[37] When you are overwhelmed and your spirit grows faint, I bless you with the assurance that He knows the way that you should go.[38] I bless you

---

35   John 17:20-23.
36   Acts 18:25; Romans 12:11; 1 Corinthians 7:34.
37   Isaiah 57:15.
38   Psalm 142:3.

with the confidence that when you call for help, our Father God of your spirit hears you, because He is close to the broken-hearted and rescues those who are crushed in spirit.[39] I bless your spirit with being refreshed by others who are faithful to you, and I bless you with often being a refreshment to others in their spirits[40] .... I bless you with glorifying Jesus in your body and your spirit, which are God's, because you are bought with a price.[41] I bless you with praying and singing and praising God with your spirit.[42] I bless you with exalting the Lord and rejoicing in God your Saviour with your spirit as you celebrate His choosing you and recall all the great things, He has done for you.[43] I bless you with worshipping our Father God in spirit and truth.[44] I bless you in the name of our Father God of the spirits of all mankind.[45] [46]

---

39 Psalm 34:18.

40 1 Corinthians 16:18, 2 Corinthians 7:13.

41 1 Corinthians 6:20 NKJV.

42 1 Corinthians 14:14-16.

43 Luke 1:46-49.

44 John 4:23-24.

45 Numbers 16:22.

46 Blessing Your Spirit – With The Blessings of Your Father And The Names of God, Sylvia Gunter, Arthur Burk p 152 Publisher: Our Father Gods Business, Birmingham, Alabama 2005.

SECTION 2

OUR VICTORY IN CHRIST JESUS

"Therefore, put on the full armour of God, so that when the day of evil comes, you may be able to stand your ground, and after you have done everything, to stand."

Ephesians 6:13

Chapter 2.1

Avoiding Spiritual Abuse

"Therefore encourage [admonish, exhort] one another and edify
[strengthen and build up] one another, just as you are doing."
1 Thessalonians 5: 11 AMPC

Spiritual Abuse

It is easy for any of us to slide into spiritually abusing a person in any of our everyday relationships but particularly so when helping others on any of the roads to healing. Spiritual abuse causes extreme emotional and spiritual harm with the potential for the person to turn their back on any further relationship with God.

We need to be especially careful when we are helping others to be free from the influences and effects of evil spirits so I have chosen to raise the issue now before we engage in the specifics of how satan, the enemy of our souls, can affect and influence us adversely. What follows are some of the specific and subtle ways in which we may slide into spiritually abusing a person.

Through imposing our views upon another

David Johnson and Jeff Van Vonderen[47] describe one form of spiritual abuse in this way,

> *It's possible to become so determined to defend a spiritual place of authority, doctrine or a way of doing things that you wound and abuse anyone who questions or disagrees or doesn't 'behave' spiritually the way you want them to. When your words and actions tear down another, or attack or weaken a person's standing as a Christian to gratify you, your position or your beliefs while at the same time weakening or harming another – that is spiritual abuse.*

When we relate to others with the Spirit of Jesus[48] we can both encourage and strengthen at the one time. Exhortation under the clear leading of the Holy Spirit points the person to the words of Jesus, allowing the Holy Spirit freedom to work in the person's life. There is no sense of condemnation felt and the person is restored. Conversely, it is potentially harming to throw texts at a person when the person is not ready to receive that specific truth. Only the Spirit of God knows what the person can receive, and how and when. In Proverbs we are offered this wisdom,

> *"The intelligent person restrains his words, and one who keeps a cool head is a man of understanding."* Proverbs 17:27 HCSB

Causing others to depend on us instead of on Jesus

David Johnson & Jeff Van Vonderen suggest that people learn to be victimised or are made powerless through experiencing relationships

---

47   The Subtle Power of Spiritual Abuse: Recognizing and Escaping Spiritual Manipulation and False Spiritual Authority within the Church, David Johnson and Jeff VanVonderen, Bethany House Publishers, Repackaged Edition (1 October 2005).

48   Galatians 5:22-23.

that either have prepared them to be abused, or not prepared them to not be abused. Such relationships could be labelled "shame-based" relationships,

> *"Shame-based relationships are relationships based on shame:
> You are so weak and defective that you are nothing without this
> relationship. Shame becomes the glue that holds things together. It
> is the force that motivates people to refrain from certain behaviours
> and to do others."*[49]

Some people who come for help are particularly vulnerable to becoming dependent on those who pray with them. There is a tendency to look towards the one praying rather than to Jesus. It is wise for us to think about ways in which we "can be less and Jesus can be more."[50]

Manipulation and Control

Relationships and behaviours can be manipulated by very powerful innuendos and verbal codes that others are supposed to decode. For example, phrases like, "Don't you think it would be better this way?" are frequently used to control a person into agreeing with you. Think about some of the effects upon a person who is manipulated or controlled. How can we recognise manipulation or control in ourselves?

Preoccupation with fault and blame

This can occur where the person helping another believes that repentance and/or forgiveness is necessary and pushes this in an

---

49   The Subtle Power of Spiritual Abuse: Recognizing and Escaping Spiritual Manipulation and False
     Spiritual Authority within the Church, David Johnson and Jeff VanVonderen, p 55, Bethany House
     Publishers, Repackaged Edition (1 October 2005).

50   John 3:30.

abusive way. We must not let our zeal for a person's freedom overtake wisdom and sensitivity. It is wise to think about how these issues can be approached by focussing on the well-being of the other person and truly listening to how they're expressing themselves. We all need to be encouraged to develop an understanding of ourselves with the help of revelation from God so that we can explore values and truth for ourselves. Love and affirmation of the person provides a safe environment in which they can explore such issues.

We can focus on Jesus in prayer, asking for help as we listen to the person and as they explain the problem to us. We can ask Jesus to lead us in prayer and when we are given words of knowledge, not flaunt them but quietly and gently pursue the revelation. We are there to care for the person through providing a place of unconditional love and acceptance, letting Jesus be the focus and the Healer. It is good to keep reminding ourselves,

> *"Not by might nor by power but by My Spirit, says the Lord of Hosts."* Zechariah 4:6

Terminology

As we move into discussing the effects and influences of the different evil realms it is important for us to remember that all evil spirits aim to steal, kill and destroy, to divide and conquer, to pull down and shame. Anyone with an evil spirit influencing them needs patient unconditional love and acceptance. Our prayer should be that just as God helps us to become aware of any destructive behaviours so He will help others.

Sadly, the presence of an evil spirit in a person may not only be disempowering and traumatic for that person but can also affect others in their circle of acquaintances. Thus, there can be a dynamic of "perpetrator" and "victim". In using these terms as descriptions, I am aware that the "perpetrator" as well as the "victim" is troubled. I am not using it in a condemnatory way but merely to distinguish behaviours in this process of setting people free.

Chapter 2.2

Our Victory over Evil

"And the God of peace will swiftly pound satan to a pulp under your feet! And the wonderful favour of our Lord Jesus will surround you."
Romans 16:20

When I first heard of the ministry of deliverance about fifty years ago, I didn't want anything to do with it. Little did I understand at that time just how important a ministry this is and, ten years later, when I answered God's call to set the captives free, I discovered just how wonderful it is to partner with Him in bringing freedom to people from the harassment of the evil around and within us which is caused by satan and his fallen kingdom. It is important that with God's help we seek to understand the working of our enemy and to be aware of some of the different ways in which he can have a hold over our lives and how we might be released from those holds. Jesus called it,

"bringing liberty to the captives." Luke 4:18

We remember that God is the creator and is everywhere at once whereas satan is a created being and can only be in one place at a time. Any spiritual battle is not one between equals.

The War of Two Worlds

So far, in seeking restoration of body, soul and spirit we have considered our need of repentance, the necessity of forgiving others, and the importance of bringing every thought captive in obedience to Christ. We have discussed Inner Healing and Physical Healing. In this section we will discuss the need to take account of the fact that we have a common enemy who seeks to steal, kill and destroy us as God's people,

> *"For our struggle is not against flesh and Blood, but against the rulers, against the authorities, against the powers of this dark world and against the spiritual forces of evil in the heavenly realm."* Ephesians 6:12

The battle is between us and the evil around us which aims to destroy our freedom in Christ. Paul writes in his letter to the believers in the Ephesian Church that this battle can only be fought by spiritual means because our enemy is spirit,

> *"For though we live in the world we do not wage war as the world does. The weapons we fight with are not the weapons of the world. On the contrary they have divine power to demolish strongholds."* 2 Corinthians 10:3-4

Strongholds are patterns of long-established thinking that are difficult to change. We will be discussing how to demolish these false mind-sets in the next chapter but, first, we will consider why we have such a battle.

We read in the Bible that as well as a natural, physical world there is an invisible, spiritual world. God is Spirit, living beyond time and space in this spiritual world in which there are other spirit beings, both good and evil. He created us in His likeness as spirit and with a soul and a physical body. As God's people, we live in both worlds, the physical and the spiritual.[51]

From scripture we understand that God created angels to live with Him and to serve Him in His kingdom. The three most notable were Lucifer the worshipper, Michael the warrior and Gabriel the messenger. Seraphim, cherubim, and angels are also mentioned.

Over time, Lucifer became prideful, wanting to be the centre of worship, and so rebelled against God. As a consequence, he and a third of all the angels who aligned with his delusions were thrown out of heaven by God. Since this eviction Lucifer is known as satan and his followers as evil spirits or demons. It is widely held that a fairly full picture of the origin of satan and his demons is described in Ezekiel 28:11-19 and Isaiah 14:12-17. Jesus gave an eyewitness account of the eviction of satan from heaven in Luke 10:18 and Revelation 12:7-9 due to his sin and God's judgment on him.

He and his hierarchy of evil spirits aim to kill, steal and destroy what God has created. Since he has been defeated by Jesus at the cross, he knows that he cannot win any battle against Him and so focusses his attention on God's created people, determined to destroy them and their relationship with God their heavenly Father. He wants to stop people from becoming followers of Christ or from being effective as Christians.[52] This is why we have a battle but it is one that Jesus has won for us at the Cross. Once we understand this and make a stand in Jesus' name we can no longer be adversely influenced.

Jesus makes it clear that satan is a king with a kingdom,

> *"And if satan cast out satan, he is divided against himself; how then shall his kingdom stand?"* Matthew 12:26

---

51 Ephesians 2:6.
52 Romans 6:6,11.

In this kingdom there is a hierarchy of evil which Paul refers to as principalities, powers, and rulers of the darkness of this age[53] which have thrones and dominions[54].

In Genesis we read that when God created Adam, He gave him dominion over the earth and its creatures. When Eve, and then Adam, listened to and were lured into believing and following the deceptive words of the serpent (Lucifer in disguise) they disobeyed God and submitted to the rule of satan. As a consequence satan took from them the authority over the earth which God had given them. Paul writes that he is *"the god of this world"*[55] John writes, *"we know that we are children of God, and that the whole world is under the control of the evil one"* 2 John 5:19.

This evil one aims to deceive, accuse, disturb, distress, bring despair, depress and destroy God's people but he can only succeed in as far as we allow. Some people are so afraid of the mention of an evil spirit that they would rather ignore the possibility, something which pleases satan as he can then trespass on their lives for as long as he chooses. He is a finite being and can only be in one place at a time so he has to use his army of evil spirits to do his work over the world. According to scripture these evil spirits or demons oppose all aspects of the blessings of God's kingdom. They are referred to as unclean spirits, deaf and dumb spirits, spirits of infirmity, bondage, slumber, fear, jealousy etc.

What about the Good News?

Jesus had a personal encounter with satan in the wilderness at the time of His temptations[56] and, in overcoming, He established for

---

53   Ephesians 6:12.
54   Colossians 1:16.
55   2 Corinthians 4:4.
56   Matthew 4:1-11.

all time "His moral ascendancy over the evil one".[57] From that time satan's freedom was limited as he now knew that in any showdown Jesus would have the upper hand. At the time when Jesus predicted His own death, He had this to say,

> *"Now is the time for judgement on this world; now the prince of this world will be driven out."* John 12:31

At the cross Jesus as a man fulfilled this when He overcame death and defeated satan once and for all, taking back the authority that had been stolen from man in the Garden of Eden. Since then, satan has turned his attention to working against Jesus indirectly through people, and through powers and the elements. He and his followers continue trying to gain authority over the lives of people by any means, perhaps through using deception, accusation or condemnation,

> *"Your enemy the devil prowls around like a roaring lion looking for someone to devour."* 1 Peter 5:8

As followers of Jesus the only authority satan and evil spirits gain over us is what we allow them to have. The presence of Jesus within us repels evil spirits and, when in Jesus' name we use the authority that we have been given, they have to obey. I remember on one occasion that an evil spirit came at me determined to choke me but was stopped in its track as soon as it came close. It was a bit nerve-wracking at the time but showed me very clearly how protected I was. On another occasion taking authority over an evil spirit stopped the spirit from propelling the person out the door of the room and down steep winding stairs. The potential for an accident was high. When we face any evil spirit in the authority of Jesus' name, we discover how small and lacking in power it is compared to a child of God who stands against it in the name of Jesus.

---

57 Binding and Loosing, Tom Marshall, Hodder and Stoughton.

The work of Jesus in removing the hold that this enemy has on mankind is to be continued in this age by His followers through exercising His authority in His name by the power of His Spirit,[58]

"I tell you the truth, anyone who has faith in Me will do what I have been doing. He will do even greater things than these because I am going to the Father." John 14:12

As we learn in Ephesians 3:10 it is through the Church that God reveals His manifold wisdom to the rulers and authorities in the heavenly realms. When evil entities attack the Church, they can be pushed back through the presence and power of God wherever there is unity of the spirit.[59] It is the love of God that causes evil to leave, not just skill and knowledge.

Whenever we need insight from God, we can expect to receive it through the Holy Spirit who is, "the spirit of truth"[60] and, "the spirit of wisdom and revelation",[61]

"The Sovereign Lord has given me a well-instructed tongue, to know the word that sustains the weary. He wakens me morning by morning, wakens my ear to listen like one being instructed." Isaiah 50:4

When we receive insight, we also receive faith to overcome.[62] God often sends His angels to be ministering spirits to serve us in this work.[63] In Christ we already have the victory over evil but we must enforce it if we are to live in freedom.

---

58   Binding and Loosing, Tom Marshall, Hodder and Stoughton.
59   Psalm 133, Ephesians 4:13.
60   1 John 4:6.
61   Ephesians 1:17.
62   2 Corinthians 4:13.
63   Hebrews 1:14.

Setting the Captives Free

Under the Old Covenant, although there may have been deliverance from evil spirits through obedience, no-one had authority to command demons to stop harassing a person. While Jesus was walking the earth, He was recognized as One who spoke with authority[64] and who exerted His authority over satan and his demons, sometimes healing people through setting them free from evil spirits,

> *"Jesus healed many who had various diseases. He also drove out many demons."* Mark 1:34

He commissioned His disciples to continue His work of freeing the captives,

> *"When Jesus had called the Twelve together, He gave them power and authority to drive out all demons and to cure all diseases, and He sent them out to preach the kingdom of God and to heal the sick."* Luke 9:1-2

and later sent out the seventy-two who returned with joy saying,

> *"Lord, even the demons submit to us in Your name."* Luke 10:17

Jesus' response is significant,

> *"I saw satan fall like lightning from heaven. I have given you authority to trample on snakes and scorpions, and to overcome all the power of the enemy; nothing will harm you. However, do not rejoice that the spirits submit to you, but rejoice that your names are written in heaven."* Luke 10:18-20

---

64   Luke 4.

Early on in my involvement in this ministry I clearly remember being excited by and thanking Jesus for a deliverance that had set someone free. His gentle response was, "don't rejoice that the demons submit to you. Rejoice that your name is written in heaven". I felt such deep gratitude welling up inside me. How wonderful to know that our names are written in heaven.

Demons can affect a believer from outside them or from within if there has been an opening given through ancestral rights, through trauma or through the person's own sins. Once a person receives Jesus as Lord and Saviour, and is filled with the Holy Spirit, nothing of an evil nature can reside within their spirits because they have been renewed by the Holy Spirit. However, until freed, there can be oppression coming from demonic around or within their souls or bodies. These, together with their influences and effects, can be readily removed through the finished work of Jesus in His name, and the areas vacated subsequently filled with the Holy Spirit,

> *"Having disarmed principalities and powers, He made a public spectacle of them, triumphing over them in it."* Colossians 2:15

Oppression is not possession. There is nothing in original Greek to justify putting the word "possessed" alongside the word "demons". The correct translation is to have an unclean or evil spirit affecting and influencing us.[65] A Christian cannot be possessed by demons but can be under the influence of or have an evil spirit, for example, Ananias and Sapphira.[66] It is unlikely that a person is possessed by an evil spirit unless they have deliberately made a choice to make satan their lord and even then, if that person comes to faith in Jesus, they can be set free. Jesus is Lord over all. Anyone can be affected or oppressed by evil spirits around them whether they are Christian or

---

65   Matthew 11:18.
66   Acts 5:3.

not and, again, this is easily stopped by using our authority in Jesus' name. Frequently, a person is aware when they are being so affected.

Examples of evil spirits harassing people are numerous. An indication of this as a possibility is where a person has repented of and is persevering in trying to overcome some sin yet feels driven repeatedly back into that sin. Evil spirits seek to drive or push a person into harmful patterns of thinking or behaviour whereas God doesn't force but gently invites and leads. The enemy of our souls can only gain territory or oppress us to the extent that he has been allowed entry through sin or by invitation, whether by us or our ancestors, so it is incumbent on us to live responsibly. When we move away from a sinful habit any evil spirit associated with it leaves gradually over time or can be evicted immediately in the name of Jesus.

Some Signs that an Evil Spirit may be Hindering a Person from Gaining Freedom

- being stuck at a point in spiritual development despite prayerful obedience

- emotional problems that persist or recur

- mental problems that are disturbances in the mind or thought life, such as mental torment, confusion, etc.

- speech problems such as lying, blasphemy, criticism, mockery, and gossip

- attitudes and behaviour such as jealousy, bitterness and anger

- sexual problems such as recurring unclean thoughts and acts regarding sex, including fantasy sex experiences

- addictions to nicotine, alcohol, drugs, medicines, food etc.

- physical illness and diseases which have been caused by spirits of infirmity.[67] Not all sicknesses are.

- spiritual error as found in cults and secret societies can open the door for demons

- tormenting fears

- irrational thoughts

- compulsion to destructive acts

- feelings of lifelessness or of being shut down

- preoccupation with specifics

- blockages or bondages causing lack of freedom or peace

- especially strong negative reactions to the idea of deliverance

Note that there can be many different reasons for any of the above. Evil spirits or demons are one possibility but so are our own sins and wounds.[68] We must not jump to conclusions but seek God's insight.

What are Footholds, sometimes called Legal Rights?

A foothold is an opening in our lives that can give evil spirits an opportunity to harass us. They can gain entry through ingrained ungodly thinking, attitudes or inner vows, through fear and idolatry, through sexual and other sin. In scripture we are urged to deal with sin as quickly as possible for our own good as well as for the good of others.[69] Some footholds have been given by family members in a previous generation but these, too, can be stopped. Some of the most common footholds are now described.

---

67   Luke 13:11.

68   Breaking Through Barriers to Blessing, Overcoming Sins, Wounds and Demons, David Legge, Malcolm Down Publishing, 2017.

69   Ephesians 4:27-32.

Generational or Ancestral Sins[70]

Persistent sin in any area opens a person up to the possibility of being tormented by an evil spirit associated with that sin. Perhaps you have been aware of a family in which someone has a problem such as uncontrollable anger and their father or mother and grandfather or grandmother are similarly affected. This is an example of how evil spirits can be passed down from generation to generation until the sin is repented of (behaviour changed to align with scripture) and the spirit removed. Not only can propensity to certain sins be passed down through the generations in this way but so can some sicknesses whether mental, physical or spiritual. Sicknesses that are generational may be, but are not always, the consequence of sin in the lives of forebearers. Jesus made this clear when He healed the man blind from birth,

> *"His disciples asked him, 'Rabbi, who sinned, this man or his parents, that he was born blind?' 'neither this man nor his parents sinned,' said Jesus."* John 9:2-3

As we read the story of the healing of the boy with an evil spirit in Mark 9:17-27, we notice that the boy was affected from childhood. Jesus asked questions, established the root, called for faith, and then cast out the demon and forbade it to return. He did not ask the boy to repent. It's worth noting that later when talking to His disciples He made it clear that some deliverances may require prayer and fasting.[71]

There are many people today who are living under such bondages. In a Christian this does not mean that they are not saved but that they are not free. What has the Bible to say with regard to this? Under the Old Covenant we read this about God,

---

70   Some of the material in this section is taken from greatbiblestudy.com: "Generational curses."
71   Matthew 17:19-21.

"...maintaining love to thousands, and forgiving wickedness, rebellion and sin. Yet He does not leave the guilty unpunished; He punishes the children and their children for the sin of the fathers to the third and fourth generation." Exodus 34:7

"Our ancestors sinned and are no more, and we bear their punishment. Slaves rule over us, and there is no one to free us from their hands." Lamentations 5:7-8

There were times when the nation of Israel bore the consequences of the sins of the fathers, for example through being exiled to Babylon. Scripture also records that at the end of the allotted seventy years of exile, Daniel repented on behalf of the people pleading for God's mercy,[72] and that subsequently God used King Cyrus to allow them to return to their land.[73]

An example of sin being passed down through the generations is seen in the stories of Abraham and succeeding generations. Having gone to Egypt because of famine in the land, he was afraid that the Egyptians would kill him so that they could take Sarai, who was beautiful, so he thought up a plan,

"Please say you are my sister, that it may be well with me for your sake, and that I may live because of you." Genesis 12:13

The truth was that she was his half-sister, but, more importantly, she was his wife. Using half-truths is deception. We can observe the consequences of this sin of deception passing down through the generations from Abraham. Isaac pretended Rebekah wasn't his wife. Jacob deceived his father to get the birth-right due his brother. Laban deceived Jacob. Jacob deceived Laban and then was deceived by some of his sons with respect to his son, Joseph. David deceived to cover

---

72 Daniel 9:1-17.
73 Ezra 1:1-4.

up his sin with Bathsheba. His son, Absalom deceived him. Ahab deceived to get Naboth's vineyard. In these accounts we see a sorry picture of man's sinfulness. It is worth observing that when sin has not been repented of, and the consequences handed on from generation to generation that there is the possibility of increasing evil. Scripture seems to suggest this with reference to Omri and his son, Ahab who was even more evil than he,

"But Omri did evil in the eyes of the Lord and sinned more than all those before him.... Ahab son of Omri did more evil in the eyes of the Lord than any of those before him." 1 Kings 16:25, 30

However, Jeremiah prophesied of a time that was to come under the New Covenant when this would all change,

"In those days people will no longer say, 'The fathers have eaten sour grapes, and the children's teeth are set on edge.' Instead, everyone will die for his own sin; whoever eats sour grapes, his own teeth will be set on edge." Jeremiah 31:29-30

and Paul wrote,

"Christ redeemed us from the curse of the law by becoming a curse for us, for it is written: Cursed is everyone that hanged on a tree." Galatians 3:13

We remember that Jesus came full of grace and truth[74] and where truth is received the grace of God enters a repentant heart. Because Christ was made a curse, we can be freed from the curses that sins have brought upon us. What does this mean for us in terms of the consequences of generational sin being passed on to new generations, and in terms of personal sin? Because of what Jesus did in paying the

---

74 John 1:14 NET.

price for our sin, those who are in Christ will not be denied eternal life either because of our own sin or our forefathers' sin. We will not "die". Those who are in Christ are redeemed and forgiven and have the promise of eternal life. However, in this life, we may live with the consequences of that sin until we actively seek and receive freedom in Jesus' name. This is guaranteed because Jesus took our place and became a curse for us.

The consequence of generational sin in our lives can be most easily seen where there is a recurring pattern throughout the generations e.g., illness such as depression, heart problems, cancer etc, a pattern of "being robbed" financially, persistent irrational fears, negative attitudes such as bitterness. Anything that seems to be a persistent struggle or problem and is evident from one generation to another may, but not always, be the consequence of sin that has not been repented of in a previous generation. Demons don't automatically leave our souls and bodies when we become Christians any more than sin does. If we think we are struggling as a result of the consequences of sin in our family line, we can go to Jesus to be set free. The good news is that if this is before we have any children and also while our children are still dependent on us, we can pray for them to be freed at the same time as ourselves.

The prophecy of Jeremiah in chapter 31:29-30 makes it clear that God's people are not to excuse themselves from their own sin by blaming a previous generation. They are to take responsibility for their own sin. An example of this is King David who expressed repentance for his own sin in Psalm 51:1-4. In Jesus' name we can break the power of the consequences of generational sin and release ourselves from its propensity to drive us to sin because Jesus shed His Blood on our behalf,

> *"For you know that it was not with perishable things such as silver or gold that you were redeemed from the empty way of life handed*

down to you from your ancestors, but with the precious Blood of
Christ, a lamb without blemish or defect." 1 Peter 1:18-19

Generational negative influences may lie dormant until awakened by
some trigger. This can happen when God chooses to expose some
hidden demonic oppression so that we can be set free with His help.
Sometimes, satan may try to thwart us in the calling God has placed
on our lives by choosing a strategic time in which to awaken latent
sin together with demonic that has a generational root. If we pray
consistently asking God to expose any inherent sin in our lives, He
will reveal these so that we can resolve them with His help.

Rather than becoming disillusioned by the effects of generational sin
in our lives, let us strengthen ourselves with the sure knowledge of
our victory in Christ over all sinfulness, and of our assured promise
of abundant life as we take possession of all that Jesus has won for
us on the Cross. Let us remember, too, that just as the effects of
sinfulness in the generations may be passed on, so, also, the effects
of godly living. A godly heritage is empowering and deserving of
immense gratitude.

Curses

A curse leading to some form of misfortune may be directed at one
or more persons, a place, or an object. Examples of such objects are
idols, occult books and rings, some films and charms. Land can also
become defiled by the sins of its owners.[75]

A curse can be put into effect through the spoken word or through
some kind of spell or ritual in black magic or witchcraft. When used
within the context of witchcraft it may be called a hex or jinx. It is

---

75 Leviticus 18:27.

made effective through evil spirits. A person can unknowingly curse another if their words spoken to the person do not align with what they're thinking in their hearts and saying to others about that person. It is also possible to curse ourselves as a consequence of our own thought life (self-curse). This was discussed in Book 1, chapter 2.2 of this series.

Curses caused by ungodly words and attitudes may be directed at the person themselves or have been passed down through their generational line, for example Genesis 9:24-25,

> *"And Noah awoke from his wine, and knew what his younger son had done unto him. And he said, 'Cursed be Canaan; a servant of servants shall he be unto his brethren.'"*

Scripture records that this curse eventually affected an entire nation.

We may become aware of a curse against us because the Holy Spirit alerts us but we don't always need to know the specifics. For example, someone who had been struggling with tiredness for eight weeks came for prayer. When we asked God about it, we were told it was the result of a curse. After we had prayed to break her free from the curse together with its influences and effects, she immediately felt her energy restored and became alert.

If we notice a destructive generational pattern of misfortune such as frequent car accidents, poverty despite adequate income, tendency towards a specific illness etc., we can seek the Holy Spirit's insight as to whether a curse is in place.

Scripture tells us that a curse without cause cannot land,

> *"Like a fluttering sparrow or a darting swallow, an undeserved curse does not come to rest."* Proverbs 26:2

However, just as a fluttering sparrow or darting swallow can leave unpleasant deposits behind which need to be cleaned up, so also can a curse leave its extremely unpleasant effects and influences on a person from which they will need releasing.

Curses need to be renounced and broken and forgiveness released. In Jesus' name, the person can be severed from the curse together with its influences and effects, and any associated evil spirit commanded to leave. They can then ask God to heal them from the effects and influences of the curse.

Strongholds

This subject will be discussed fully in the next chapter, *Strongholds (Deep-Rooted Ungodly Thinking and Behaviour)*.

Unforgiveness

When we don't forgive others, we may give the enemy a foothold in our lives. Jesus calls it being handed over to the tormentors.[76]

Ungodly soul and spirit ties

Under the old covenant God entreated His people to live separately from those who followed idolatrous worship and was ruthless against ungodly alliances because of the consequent evil effect on His people. As history reveals, they often did not heed the warning and, as a consequence, turned away from God.[77] Under the new covenant Paul urges the Corinthians,

---

76   Matthew 18:23-35.
77   2 Chronicles 20:35-37.

"Come out from them and be separate." 2 Corinthians 6:17

This command was in the context of advising God's people not to come into agreement with the idolatry that was around them. Previously he had written,

> *"Do not be deceived and misled! Evil companionships corrupt and deprave good manners and morals and character."* 1 Corinthians 15:33

This does not mean that we are to have nothing to do with those outside the kingdom of God but, rather, that we are not to associate with their ideas and come into agreement with them. Other scriptures are Proverbs 22:5, 24-25; Haggai 2:12-14.

Soul and spirit tie are connections, soul and spirit, between two or more people and can be good and holy, or bad and evil. Good soul and spirit ties are based upon the "royal law" of love,[78] also called the "law of Christ".[79] Thus godly (good) ties represent the bonding together of people with "agape" love, love that is unconditional and serves. Some good ties can be seen in parents with their children,[80] spouses,[81] friends[82] and Christian brothers and sisters.[83] Christ is the head of the Church and as each member is joined to the Lord by the one Spirit so Godly ties are formed.

There are many ways in which we can form ungodly soul and spirit ties with a person. All are the consequence of coming into an agreement which is ungodly in that it does not align with God's kingdom principles. Ungodly ties are formed by any spirit which protects "self",

---

78 James 2:8.
79 Galatians 6:2.
80 Genesis 44:20.
81 Ephesians 5:28.
82 1 Samuel 18:1.
83 Ephesians 5:1-2.

for example, pride, control, anger, jealousy, lust. They are formed through ungodly unions such as control, adultery and fornication.[84] A good soul and spirit tie brings life, and a bad one, death.

Whatever we are connected to sources what we receive, and so it is vital that we are only connected to the true Source. Once ungodly ties are formed between two or more people these people become bound together in some unhealthy way, each holding a part of the other person or people emotionally and spiritually. Demons tormenting one person may torment others and so no-one is able to move with freedom of choice under God. God helps us by speaking to us through His Word,

> *"For the word of God is alive and active. Sharper than any double-edged sword, it penetrates even to dividing soul and spirit, joints and marrow; it judges the thoughts and attitudes of the heart."* Hebrews 4:12

Often when one person in a relationship is set free spiritually it has a knock-on effect in the spiritual world for the good of the other.

To become free a person may possibly have to forgive the other person in some way, for example, forgive the person who is controlling them. Then they will need to repent of their part in it through colluding with the ungodly behaviour and choose to change. Finally, in Jesus' name they can cut any ungodly soul and spirit ties with that person in relation to the ungodly behaviour (in this example, control) and ask Jesus to return to each person what belongs to them and to cleanse the relationship with the Blood of Jesus. This leaves each free to re-establish the relationship on a Godly basis. Only then can any evil spirit associated with this be commanded to leave in Jesus' name. We need to be as specific as possible. As God's people we can avoid such

---

84   1 Corinthians 6:16

ungodly ties by praying, "Lord Jesus, today I pray that the only soul and spirit ties that I form will be through You".

Childhood Hurt or Abuse

Much demonic bondage is caused during childhood. For example, if a child repeatedly feels rejected by their parents however unintentional a spirit of rejection may reinforce the child's thinking.

Points of Vulnerability

Examples are emotional or physical shock or trauma, fearful experiences especially during childhood, or through alcoholism, drugs and gambling.

Cult and Occult involvement

Any source of activity that opposes the truth as taught in scripture leads us away from God towards destruction and death.[85]

When a person joins a cult, they form ungodly ties with every member of the cult, are not free to make choices, and may find it difficult to leave. It is as though an invisible spiritual rope attaches each person to every other (ungodly soul and spirit ties). By means of this rope each can be controlled, or have an ungodly power over others, either through the flesh or through evil spirits. Both have responsibility, whether they are controlling or being controlled. In prayer for release the person needs to pray as above, severing all ungodly ties they have with each and every member of the cult in Jesus' name.

---

85 Acts 17: 24-31.

There are many different occultic practices each of which is a pathway that takes us away from God into activities that endanger our souls. Examples are playing the Ouija board or participating in occult activities such as a séance.

Demonic vows can be made deliberately or unintentionally. Joining a cult or a secret society often involves taking vows. Participating in such activities can open the door to evil spirits. James urges us,

> *"do not swear-not by heaven or by earth or by anything else. Let your 'Yes' be 'Yes' and your 'No' be 'No', or you will be condemned."* James 5:12

Once a person joins a cult, they may be given a spirit guide. These are evil spirits to which the person looks for guidance instead of looking to God, the source of all we need,

> *"His divine power has given us everything we need for a godly life through our knowledge of him who called us by his own glory and goodness."* 2 Peter 1:3

Trances can be brought on by a person or an object e.g., through repeating key words or through eye contact. A person can protect themselves from being tranced by abiding in Christ because the love of Jesus is stronger than death and can withstand any attempt to bring on such a trance.

A person can also bring trance upon themselves through witchcraft practices, especially where they have been familiar with them as they grew up. For example, one person cursed herself by drawing a circle around herself and praying in demonic tongues, another through cursing herself with a witchcraft sign. As the trance began to take effect, each could feel paralysis creeping over their bodies. As with every form of ministry we follow the leading of the Holy Spirit to set the person free.

Freedom from Captivity (Deliverance)

Although there are many ways in which satan attempts to hinder us in our lives there is one route to freedom and that is through Jesus. The deliverance ministry is for Christians and for those who will become Christians through it. When we remove an evil spirit in Jesus' name it is important to ask the Holy Spirit to fill the place previously occupied by that evil spirit and to close the door. Otherwise, it will return, find its home empty and clean, and invite seven other wicked spirits to join it in occupying the vacant space.[86] This will leave the person in a worse state. While there are some basic principles that are present in the process leading to deliverance there are usually some details specific to ministry for each person which only the Holy Spirit can reveal.

Jesus, His disciples and the Apostles were not afraid of satan. Neither should we be. In scripture, we are given many insights as to how to resist evil in our lives.[87] Our part is to live humbly in dependence on God, living free in the light of scriptural truth while receiving God's grace to help us. We must take captive any ungodly thoughts, repent of (turn away from) any transgression and forgive any wrong done to us. Sometimes we deal with a symptom rather than deal with the problem that caused the symptom, for example when we forgive as an act of obedience (cognitive) without engaging with God so that He can remove the hurt inflicted (heart). Deliverance occurs when we remove the source that gave an open door in our lives to the enemy's influence. Jesus assures us of authority in His name and power through the Holy Spirit to enable us to become free. This is summed up by Peter,

---

86   Matthew 12:45.
87   1 Corinthians 10:4-5; Ephesians 4:27, 6:11; James 4:7-8,10; 1 Peter 5:8 etc.

"Humble yourselves, therefore, under God's almighty hand, that He may lift you up in due time. Cast all your anxiety on Him for He cares for you. Be self-controlled and alert. Your enemy the devil prowls around like a roaring lion looking for someone to devour. Resist him, standing firm in the faith." 1 Peter 5:6-9

Steps that lead towards Freedom from Oppression by Evil Spirits

When Jesus returned to Nazareth, He entered the synagogue and proclaimed,

"The Spirit of the Lord is on Me, because He has anointed Me to preach the good news to the poor. He has sent Me to proclaim freedom to the prisoners and recovery of sight for the blind, to release the oppressed, to proclaim the year of the Lord's favour." Luke 4:18,19

In response to these claims, He was thrown out of the synagogue and, despite attempts made to kill Him, walked away. In contrast when He arrived in Capernaum and entered the synagogue there, He was recognised for His authority in teaching and for His power when an impure spirit was ordered to leave a man.[88]
Many other examples of Jesus' authority and power over evil spirits are recorded in scripture, e.g., He released a woman who had been crippled by an evil spirit for eighteen years[89] and the Gerasene demoniac from many impure spirits.[90]

In terms of bringing release to the captives He often began by asking the person what they wanted. Whether seeking freedom for ourselves or for others, being able to voice a specific request gives focus as to what we really want. Sometimes when an evil spirit is oppressing us

---

88 Luke 4:31-36.
89 Luke 13:16.
90 Luke 8:26-38.

it can be difficult to express our will verbally. When we understand what is hindering us, we can bind the spirit and command it to stop interfering and communicating in Jesus' name. This leaves us free to voice our desire and make choices for Jesus and against satanic bondages.

When necessary, Jesus dealt with issues such as sin, encouraging the person to change their lifestyle, and made it clear that His authority and power over demons was through the power of the Holy Spirit and evidence of the presence of the kingdom of God.[91] He was doing on earth the things that had already been done in heaven. He was doing what His Father was doing,[92] binding what needed bound and loosing what needed loosing.

Binding and Loosing

In Matthew 16:13-20, Jesus confirms that He is the Messiah, the Christ, the Son of the Living God and that He will build His church, and the gates of Hades ("the powers of death" RSV) will not prevail against it. He goes on to say,

> *"I will give you (the Church) the keys of the kingdom of heaven; whatever you bind on earth will be [will have been] bound in heaven, and whatever you loose on earth will be [will have been] loosed in heaven."* Matthew 16:19

Jesus has given us authority to use His name[93] and so every command directed at evil spirits is a command issued under the authority of Jesus who has all authority over heaven and earth.[94]

---

91   Matthew 12:28.
92   John 5:19.
93   Matthew 10:1; Mark 3:15; Luke 9:1, 10:19.
94   Matthew 28:18.

When an evil spirit is causing a sickness, we can loose ourselves from the evil spirit and ask God to heal us from its influences and effects. For example, Jesus loosed the woman from the evil spirit that had bound her for eighteen years.[95]

When an evil spirit is driving us into repeatedly committing a sin that we are trying to stop doing it is acting like a strong man in our life. We can loose ourselves from its influence by binding it. Jesus teaches about this in Matthew 12. Once we have bound the evil spirit we can plunder its house by removing its power and giving the power to Jesus, and then commanding it not to interfere or communicate with us (this is true for both generational and personal sin). This immobilises the spirit, preventing it from driving us into that sin, and so we have freedom to turn away completely from it.

If a person has bound themselves through making an inner vow (or self-imposed curse or self-fulfilling prophecy) then, after repenting, they can be loosed from that vow.[96] Loosing from occult bondage will be necessary where a person has been involved in witchcraft, spiritism, magic, pagan religions or societies.

We are to loose whatever God looses in heaven, for example, people who are in bondage, minds that are plagued by compulsive thoughts, wills that are weak in the face of addictions and enslaving habits, emotions that are affected by hurt, fear and inhibitions, bodies that suffer from physical, psychosomatic, and spiritually based sicknesses and disabilities, and relationships.

We are to bind on earth whatever God binds in heaven including circumstances and influences that oppose the will of God and actions, attitudes and influences that are instruments of evil.

---

95   Luke 13:10-17.
96   Proverbs 26:2.

On many occasions it is not necessary when talking to a person to use the words, "evil spirits" or "demons", as these terms may possibly worry some. So, for example, instead of using the phrase, "I bind the spirit of anger in Jesus' name" we can simply say, "I bind anger in Jesus' name", and then command it to leave. Always, always we bathe the person in the love of God and only do and say what is loving and kind. People often don't need to know detail that they are not prepared for. However, we don't want anyone who has repented and is trying to live free to leave a time of ministry still struggling with an issue because an evil spirit is influencing them. If you are fearful about this area of ministry, take time to, "*be still and know that I am God*" as declared in Psalm 46:10.

It is in developing this "knowing God" in the stillness, that we find our place in Him and in this world. It is in becoming still and knowing Him that we are released from all our fears and anxieties. He loves each of us so completely and deeply and does everything He can to help us as we abide in Him. He takes us forward gently, releasing the severity of our struggle little by little and replacing it with His peace. As we experience this, our trust increases and we are able to allow Him into the darkness in our lives knowing that He will not let us be overwhelmed by painful emotions. He says,

> "*Do not fear, for I have redeemed you; I have summoned you by name; you are mine. When you pass through the waters, I will be with you; and when you pass through the rivers, they will not sweep over you. When you walk through the fire, you will not be burned; the flames will not set you ablaze. For I am the Lord your God, the Holy One of Israel, your Saviour; ... Since you are precious and honoured in my sight, and because I love you, ... Do not be afraid, for I am with you.*" Isaiah 43:1-5

Whenever the need for deliverance arose, either the person themselves would be able to pinpoint the source of their struggle or the Holy

Spirit would give insight. We then chatted with the person about the process and guided them into taking ownership of it. The specific steps are outlined later in this chapter. Sometimes deliverance took place relatively easily. At other times it took greater determination. While a person was being released from an evil spirit that was harassing them, they were encouraged to weaken the evil spirit by binding it, severing it from its power in Jesus' name, and giving the power to Jesus. Doing this disempowered the spirit so that it became weak, and demonstrated to the spirit that the person had control over it and would stand against it until it left. We always commanded any evil spirit to go to the feet of Jesus and asked the Holy Spirit to come and fill the person. We then closed any doorway that had allowed entry in the first place so as to prevent re-entry. Over time we learned how to use our authority in Jesus' name with quiet confidence without the necessity for raising our voices. God gave us the amazing insight that every time we pray in this way, we lessen the power of darkness in the world.

Sometimes, after a person had been freed from an evil spirit, they were afraid that it had regained entry because they were experiencing some of what they had been freed from. This is extremely unlikely if the person is living in humble obedience. It could be that an evil spirit is hovering around the person trying to make them believe the lie so as to gain entry once again. Paul instructs us to wear the armour at all times and continue to stand against all evil.[97] We must remain alert resisting the wiles of satan.[98]

As we grew in confidence in the authority that Jesus has given us by His grace, we were directed towards delivering more powerful and resistant evil spirits. God would bring scriptures to mind which we would then read and declare to the intruder. Often the response was dramatic, and we could see that the evil spirit was "cowering" and

---

97   Ephesians 6:13.
98   1 Peter 5:8.

ready to leave. I remember vividly in the early days of this ministry that we battled for a long time to free a person from what we perceived to be a big spirit of Babylon. While taking a break and having a cuppa so that all of us could relax and have a bit of a laugh, the person we were helping suddenly was given revelation of a tiny evil spirit scuttling away across the carpet. Because of the nature of the battle this evil spirit had become larger and larger in our minds but now we were able to return with renewed energy and conviction of authority, and the intruder did indeed scuttle away.

Sometimes an evil spirit would try to hide and so we would either ask Jesus to bring it up to the surface again and not allow it to go back into hiding, or we would command that this be so in Jesus' name. Frequently, asking Jesus to surround and fill the person with His love is enough to make the spirit leave quickly. Asking the Holy Spirit to minister in the opposite spirit to that which harasses the person is effective. It is impossible for an evil spirit to remain in a person whose life is given over to Jesus and who has repented of the sin that allowed it to harass.

Throughout the process of deliverance, it is completely wrong to minister as though we are doing something for the person.

At all times we esteem the person highly, encouraging them, and discussing with them how they are feeling and what they are thinking. As we listen and discuss, and listen to God and pray, we come to an understanding together. We always work with them as a valued member of a team, maintaining their dignity and self-esteem and guarding against frightening them. We discuss each stage together so that they are prepared and ready to evict any evil spirit for themselves albeit it with us supporting them. This approach disciples them for their future and places them in a position to help others.

On any occasion that we have to step in to use our authority in helping the person we need to take care that they understand when we are addressing an evil spirit and not them. Otherwise, they can feel intimidated.

As God's children we walk in humility, depending on His leading while honouring one another. I had great joy in being alongside Reverend Jim Hagan in the ministry of deliverance. He, also, was taught and led by God and, although his insights often varied in ways from those given to me, we worked happily together, each honouring the other and learning from one another. I am the richer for having known him and partnered with him.

The Process of Deliverance

This often includes some basic principles,

- binding the strong man or evil spirit in Jesus' name and commanding it not to interfere or communicate, and then severing it from its power in Jesus' name and giving that power to the Lord Jesus

- removing footholds through repentance

- in Jesus' name commanding any evil spirit(s), one at a time, along with their influences and effects to leave and go to Jesus' feet

- after any evil spirit has left, we ask the Holy Spirit to fill the person and to close any doors that had allowed the spirit entry

The process varies slightly according to whether the presence of an evil spirit is the consequence of the person's own sin or includes the influence of this spirit coming down the generational line.

Some Further Insights

The Whisperer and the Whispering Fiend

Sometimes we can think God is speaking to us when it is actually our own voice speaking the desire of our hearts. God calls the source of this voice the whisperer.

The whisperer is the voice of the person's own heart desires mixed with deception (desires + deception). For example, one client longed so much for her male friend to fall in love with and marry her that she became convinced that God had confirmed that this would happen. In revealing the truth to her God explained that the voice she was hearing was the voice of "she who whispers", that is, her own heart. Another client who knew that there was great generational anger in both parents and who preferred to think that the anger within her was not her responsibility believed God had told her that it was an evil spirit. God revealed that it was actually her own voice that she had heard and that she needed to face her anger and deal with it.

Our own voice (the whisperer) can imprison us and deter us from living in freedom. An example could be where a person believes they can't be free and enjoy life unless someone who has hurt them acknowledges it and asks forgiveness. It can happen many times in a lifetime that hurts inflicted by another go unnoticed by the perpetrators and, even if perceived, may not be acknowledged and reconciliation sought. Sometimes a person will believe that if they are to forgive someone who has hurt them it would be like letting that person off and this, they feel, they cannot do. Yet, continuing on with unforgiveness in our hearts holds us prisoner to bitterness, self-pity and misery. As we saw earlier forgiveness sets us free from such "prisons". If we consider the life of Jesus, we see that those who flogged Him and beat Him, and those who crucified Him did not acknowledge the wrong done against Him but, despite this, Jesus forgave them and so remained free. When the offender repents before God and apologises then they too are set free.

As well as the possibility of being misled by our own whisperer we can be misled when a heart desire has been initiated by an evil spirit. God calls this voice a whispering fiend.

When we mistake either of these voices for God's voice, we can become disappointed and confused if what we think God has told us doesn't come to pass. We can also be at risk from missing out on God's best for us. Eve listened to the serpent (the whispering fiend) and chose to believe it because her own whisperer continued the internal conversation as she saw that the fruit looked good to eat and that it would give her knowledge. She allowed the desire of her heart to give rise to a whispering voice within. Because she disobeyed God, she gave her freedom (her will) over to the control of satan. She told Adam (her words to him acted in a way similar to that of a whispering fiend) and he also chose to speak to himself (the whisperer) in such a way as to disobey God. The whisperer and the whispering fiend fuel one another and so the whispering fiend knows the weaknesses and hurts of the person from the whisperer.

Familiar Spirits[99]

There are many, many different evil spirits. Sometimes a spirit may be familiar, often called a familiar spirit, because the person is so used to it being part of their lives that they are completely unaware of its presence, having adopted its thinking as their own. The person usually needs help to recognize any such intrusive thinking, and their memories should be cleansed in Jesus' name before the spirit is removed. There are several possibilities as to which evil spirits are manifesting in a person and so reliance on God is necessary if we are

---

99   1Samuel 28:7, Deuteronomy 18:10-12.

to discern what is affecting them. Two of the more unusual ones are guardian spirits such as the seer and the watcher.

Seer Spirits

The demonic version of the seer spirit sees the past, present and future. Its role is to keep the person in the past so that they never have hope for the future. In the person's thinking there is no rainbow, no hope of change from what has been. This spirit keeps the reason for their misery hidden and so prevents the person from being able to deal with past issues.

Consequently, the person remains locked into the associated feelings, apprehensions etc. from the past which have become familiar to them as part of their existence. They can neither understand for themselves what is happening nor rationalize themselves out of negativity. They struggle with hopelessness, despair and even thoughts of self-destruction.

In Book 3 of this series, we will be discussing how some people can become fragmented in their spirits and souls through extreme trauma. When this happens a part of them holding the memory of the trauma together with its associated painful emotions becomes buried and, although apparently no longer participating in life, does continue to influence their thoughts, choices and emotions. In order to illustrate the seer spirit, I make mention of one such person here. As a child this client had been subjected to excruciating acts of evil including being forced to watch her only friend being pushed out onto the road in the path of a moving car. At that time, she concluded that love was dead and resolved to "turn a blind eye" to what had happened. This had given a foothold in her life for an evil seer spirit. This spirit had remained resident in the fragmented part of her.

In ministry when God surfaced this traumatised buried part for healing, she was the age at which she had fragmented and was extremely frightened by what had happened. Once we had helped her to trust us and talk to us, we discovered that she couldn't understand what we were saying. This was a consequence of, "turning a blind eye" i.e., choosing, "not to know". "Not to know" was an inner vow made at the time which, at the beginning of her ministry, prevented her from processing anything we told her. She declared vehemently, "Love's dead".

This person part didn't know anything about the world or about sin, so we talked together about Jesus and His love for her, and about the Cross. Because she was having difficulty in understanding what I was telling her I asked Jesus what was hindering this and was told, "a seer spirit". Once this had left, she was able to grasp what was being said and could hear Jesus speak to her. He told her that He wanted her to see the sunshine and the rain with its rainbow, and to hear all the sounds like birds singing. She responded by believing what He had told her, and asking Him to forgive her for refusing to "see". She then chose to trust Him by asking Him into her life. From that point onwards she was able to understand what I was telling her about her family and other topics.

Watcher Spirits

When a watcher spirit is sent to "guard" someone, its goal is to make sure that nobody comes to help that person. The person and their needs are "hidden" from others or quickly forgotten about, and so it can appear to the person that nobody cares. Since the watcher has the ability to veil things it can stop a person from being aware of anything good that is happening in their lives and cause them to think that God is not doing anything to help them.

These two, the seer and the watcher spirits, are control spirits preventing a person from being able to rationalize what is happening.

The watcher and the seer operate from over the spirit and so hide what God is doing and interfere with a person being able to connect with God. A few years ago, I learnt that a seer and a watcher had been assigned to me to keep me on a treadmill of work. There was a continuous stream of hurting people asking for help and consequently I was busy but I loved the ministry and the joy that came in seeing God set people free and so I didn't mind. My time when not with people was spent in asking God for insights for them and in reading His word searching for insight as I listened in the Spirit. I had little time to sit and dream with Jesus. In keeping me busy these spirits had wanted to hinder me from moving forward with God in what He had planned but God had turned it around and used the opportunity to set many people free. The seer and the watcher overplayed their tactics and I was taken off the treadmill unexpectedly through having a heart attack. As a direct result I became aware of how much people cared for me and so was able to see that I was loved by many people just for being me. This new revelation changed my life dramatically and with time to rest in God's presence and seek His purpose for me in this next phase of life I have entered into so much more as Jesus has brought me into a new place with Him and into new avenues of ministry.

Demonic Imprints

When an evil spirit is expelled, it may leave an imprint of itself on the person. Imprints can be used to perpetuate symptoms that have previously been removed as a result of deliverance and healing. For example, one person was healed from fibromyalgia through deliverance from spirits of Lucifer and Ahab (discussed in chapters 2.6, 2.7) but was still having the pains and lethargy. We were given revelation that she had two imprints, one from each of these spirits. Once these were removed her healing progressed. Another was healed from an injury in her arm and was free of pain for weeks and then the pain re-appeared. God told us this was because she had an imprint of the demonic that had been removed. Through these experiences we learnt that when a person is released from an evil spirit, it is wise to command any associated imprint to leave at the same time and to cleanse the person from its influences and effects.

The enemy can use an evil spirit in one person to affect another through touching them and leaving an imprint on them. This can only happen when the evil spirit is at the surface and the person has an ungodly attitude towards the one that they are touching, and it will only land when the person who has been touched also has an ungodly attitude towards the other. Where there is disagreement between heart and mind there will be a loophole that the demonic can use. God likens this use of imprints to "call diverting". Just as a call can be diverted from a main line phone to a mobile, so the effects and influences of evil spirits can be diverted from one person to another by means of imprints. We must not fear such happenings, but remain humble and trust God to protect us as such an attitude thwarts the use of imprints.

Demonic Templates

What follows is unusual and only applicable where a person, either in a previous generation or during their own life, has been subjected to an evil that gives an opening for a demonic template to be left in some part of them. This template acts like a beacon to attract other demonic and can be there as a consequence of a generational curse or of iniquity. An example would be where such a template is used to attract demonic and thereby cause an accident. One girl came to us for prayer as she was mystified as to why she had been in four accidents in quick succession. When we asked God about it, He revealed that as a result of trauma a part of her had become buried when she was a child and that this part had a generational demonic template. On these four occasions when the girl had been driving the buried child part of her had surfaced and attracted an evil spirit which had then caused an accident. Immediately after the accident the child part with the demonic template had become buried once again leaving the person shocked and confused. We asked God to send an angel to bring the part of the person which had been buried to the surface and we removed the template in the name of Jesus. We then asked Him to release her from shock, pain and infirmity and to heal and restore her to wholeness.

When a Christian is devoted to God and seeks to give their whole life to God, repenting and forgiving day by day as God leads, then any evil spirits present will gradually weaken and leave over time. They stop harassing the person as long as the person stands resolutely against them. Paul prays,

> *"that He (God) would grant you, according to the riches of His glory, to be strengthened with power through His Spirit in the inner man."* Ephesians 3:16

and,

> *".... be strong in the Lord and in the strength of His might."*
> Ephesians 6:10

A person's ability to stand against the drive of evil is possible because Jesus dwells within them by His Spirit. As they maintain this stance evil spirits cannot influence them and if present have to leave. Although I have outlined these steps previously, I believe that they are worth repeating as repetition aids understanding.

Keeping our Eyes upon Jesus

Weapons for our Warfare[100]

- As we grow in intimate relationship with Jesus, we become convinced that God loves us personally.

- We believe that we are seated in the heavenly places above every spiritual force of wickedness

- We view all evil spirits from the perspective of heaven

- We bring every thought captive in obedience to Christ

- We remain clothed in Christ, wearing the armour of God

- We act and speak under the leading, and through the power of, the Holy Spirit

- We are entitled to speak cleansing through the Blood of Jesus

- Anything that we do or say is because of Jesus' victory over evil and, therefore, is in the name of Jesus.

Our protection comes from abiding in Christ and obeying Him. When the powers of darkness are coming against us, we can ask Father God to release the angels He has assigned to us to guard, surround and protect us. We don't need to worry when we come up against the enemy because we will always defeat him through the strength and power of the Holy Spirit and in the name of Jesus. We don't need to carry a burden on our shoulders or in our hearts but can rest in Jesus and let His authority win the battle. We are to put on the full armour of God so that we will be able to resist in the evil day, and having done everything, to stand firm against the schemes of the devil.[101] Putting on the full armour of God is equivalent to being in Christ

---

100 Ephesians 2, 6; 2 Corinthians 10.
101 Ephesians 6:10-18.

and He in us, the fullness of the character and power of God in Christ Jesus abiding in us as we abide in Him.

The Father's will is that through the Church, He might display His wisdom to confound the enemy. We have an assignment to push or hold back evil so that the Kingdom of God is advanced. As we pray in line with God's leading, we address issues and push back the advances of the enemy so that God's Spirit has freedom to move in His way. As we pray with each child of God to help them towards progressive freedom, we are praying for the Church (the people of God) that she may move progressively towards freedom under the Spirit of God. Every spirit that is removed from a person and sent to Jesus' feet is one less that the enemy can use in his war against Jesus. Every hurt or pain that is healed in a person removes a platform on which the enemy of our souls can land. Every thought taken captive in obedience to Christ is one less that the enemy can manipulate to his advantage. It is as we allow God to reveal strongholds in our lives so that they can be removed that we allow more of Jesus and His power to move in our lives,

"Stand firm then, with the belt of truth buckled around your waist, with the breastplate of righteousness in place." Ephesians 6:14a

Knowing truth as revealed by Jesus is an essential step towards deliverance and freedom. We live in the light of the truth of God's word when we apply that truth to our lives. We can then walk in truth at all times. In those areas where we have been captive to the enemy exploits, it is the truth that sets us free.

"Stand firm therefore, having put on the breastplate of righteousness." Ephesians 6:14b

We battle against the enemy, not in our own strength, but on the basis of our righteousness in Jesus. Any attempt to battle with our own efforts or out of our own thinking will be to no avail. Only God knows the battle strategy and only when clothed in the righteousness of Christ can we safely execute His commands,

"with your feet fitted with the readiness that comes from the gospel of peace." Ephesians 6:15

We battle on the basis of the Good News that Jesus defeated the enemy at the cross through His resurrection from death. The gospel of Jesus Christ is one of peace and goodwill to all men. It is a gospel of His love bringing peace where peace does not exist. This world is crying out for peace: peace within self, peace with others and peace with God. Our ministry of deliverance should have as its hallmark love, peace and power, the love of the Father as revealed through Jesus, the peace and authority that is in Christ and the ministry of power with gentleness that comes from the Holy Spirit. We are called to walk according to the Spirit[102] and so there must never be hurt caused, or accusation, or condemnation as we minister to a person. One time, while praying, God led me to pray for the church that there would be "koinonia peace" (fellowship, communion and unity in worship) which leads to unity in the Spirit. This is expressed by Paul in Colossians as unity of the Spirit in the bond of peace. Unity of the Spirit stops the enemy from breaking up relationships because he can't break a unity in the spirit that God has created.

"In addition to all this, take up the shield of faith, with which you can extinguish all the flaming arrows of the evil one." Ephesians 6:16

We battle from a place of faith in Jesus and only Jesus. He has done all that is necessary for any of us to have freedom and He is the One who will enable freedom in each of us. He has commissioned us to

---

102 Romans 8.

preach the gospel, to heal the sick and to deliver the captives and He has given us His authority in His name to enable us to do this. It is in His name that we can minister to others, and it is through His power in the Spirit that ministry is effective. It is through faith in Him that we are privileged to witness many amazing miracles of healing and deliverance. When we are ministering as a direct result of revelation and knowledge from Him, we will find that our faith in God to heal and deliver is confident and unshakeable even when there is resistance from the enemy.

"Take the helmet of salvation." Ephesians 6:17a

We succeed in this battle because we have received salvation through believing in Jesus and in what He has accomplished for us and by using,

"the sword of the Spirit, which is the word of God." Ephesians 6:17b

We defeat evil with the truth as revealed in the Word of God. Satan is legalistic and cannot stand against the truth of the Word. He and his demons may fight but they have to submit to the spoken rhema word of God, i.e., the Spirit breathed or inspired word of God. Therefore, we need to know the Word of God and be able to receive the rhema word from the Spirit. Note how often Paul urges us to stand, to stand firm, having stood to stand. We are to pray at all times in the Spirit, petitioning for the saints, be alert, and persevering. Paul ends with this statement,

"Peace to the brothers and sisters, and love with faith from God the Father and the Lord Jesus Christ. Grace to all who love our Lord Jesus Christ with an undying love." Ephesians 6:23-24

He gives us encouragement to be at peace in this battle, and to move in the love and faith that comes from God the Father and Jesus Christ.

Note that in his benediction he prays for grace for those who love the Lord Jesus Christ with an incorruptible love.

Evil spirits aim to bring chaos into a person's life. When we rebuke the demonic, we do so from the position of those who wear the shoes of the Gospel of Peace i.e., as peacemakers. Peacemakers rely on the wisdom of God in making peace.[103] The words from the Spirit are the words which pull down chaotic authority and enable peace to reign in the person. Willingness to listen to the Spirit and speak out what He says along with confidence in our position in Christ as we issue a quiet rebuke in the name of Jesus, wins the battle peaceably. Setting our faces like flint towards the goal of peace-making evicts the enemy of our souls. As we reach out for help in the name of Jesus for ourselves or for others who are captives, may God bless each of us and those to whom we minister with His love, His insight and His power.

---

103 James 3.

Chapter 2:3

Strongholds

(Deep-Rooted Ungodly Thinking and Behaviour)

"Do not conform to the pattern of this world but be transformed by the renewing of your mind. Then you will be able to test and approve what God's will is – his good, pleasing and perfect will."
Romans 12:2

What we read about as having happened physically under the old covenant has an equivalent spiritual message for us under the new covenant. Under Jehoida the Priest, evil was overthrown, Joash was made King and all followed the Lord. As a consequence, *"the city was quiet"* 2 Chronicles 23:21. Similarly when we overcome evil in the name of Jesus through enforcing the truth from the Word of God and applying the power of the Blood, we and others are set free to follow the Lord and to enjoy peace. Jesus exemplified this when faced with temptation in Luke 4.

Some of what goes on in our minds can so often not be truth. We can be subject to misperceptions, self-curses, inner vows, habits, self-protective strategies, and rationalization. We may recognize in ourselves patterns of thought, negative and damaging emotions, or critical and judgmental attitudes. Some of these we may struggle with despite trying to change.

This chapter focuses on the process of recognising and replacing thinking and beliefs that are contrary to the truth in God's Word and, where needed, removing the influence of any evil spirit behind such thinking. We mentioned previously that our hearts are the control centres of our lives and that it is what we believe in our hearts that determines how we think and behave. If our heart beliefs are false or have a tendency to negativity, we will find it difficult to receive all the blessings that God wants to give us. If through meditation on God's word His truths become rooted and grounded within our hearts then we will readily be enabled to receive all that He promises.[104]

In his letter to the church in Rome, Paul contrasted the cause and consequence of soulish thinking with that of the spiritual,

> *"The mind governed by the flesh is death, but the mind governed by the Spirit is life and peace."* Romans 8:6

As we contemplate how to change our thinking from one that is self-destructive (soulish) into one that receives life and peace (spiritual), we remember Paul's advice to the Church in Corinth,

> *"Demolish arguments and every pretension that sets itself up against the knowledge of God, and take captive every thought to make it obedient to Christ."* 2 Corinthians 10:5

Any thoughts that oppose God's Word, which Paul refers to as arguments and pretensions that set themselves against God's wisdom and insight, if allowed to persist may become strongholds in our thought life. The Greek word for stronghold is "ochuroma" which

---

104 Romans 12:2.

means "power". To hold fast is to "grip" and so a stronghold is a "power grip". A stronghold or power grip in our minds is an incorrect thinking pattern based on lies and deception which drives us in the opposite direction to that in which God wants to lead us. An example of this might be where someone has failed an important examination in the past and now thinks of themselves as a failure to such an extent that it influences their perception of their identity. A person who has grown up thinking that God is a cruel dictator may have a block to forming a relationship with Him as the Heavenly Father who loves them. These examples of two strongholds, a wrong perception of self and a wrong perception of God, are examples of the destructive nature of strongholds and extremely common.

Some examples of strongholds in scripture are:

Jealousy — Numbers 5:14; Ezekiel 8:3.
Confusion — Proverbs 23:33.
Heaviness and grief — Isaiah 61:3.
Idolatry and prostitution — 1 Corinthians 6:18, Exodus 20:14; Leviticus 26:1, 19:29; Isaiah 4:12.
Fear, torment, terror, worry, phobias — 2 Timothy 1:7.
Pride — Proverbs 16;18.
Bitterness — Hebrews 12:15.
Gossip, stubbornness, contention, arrogance, control, self-righteousness, lying — 2 Chronicles 18:22.

Our enemy named satan is described as the tempter, enticing people to sin.[105] He is the accuser of the brethren, causing anxiety with his accusations, and a deceiver, influencing our thinking against the truth of God.[106] His followers, called evil spirits or demons, join in his evil schemes. One of their main weapons is to put destructive thoughts in people's minds so as to influence them adversely and

105 Matthew 4:3.
106 Revelation 12:10-11.

then to reinforce these until they become strongholds in the person's thinking. Often this process goes unnoticed by the person as they assume the thoughts are their own.

The presence of a stronghold may be evident when those who are in Christ struggle to change thinking that they know clearly goes against God's will. Any demonic influence present acts like a force driving the person along a negative line of thinking and making it difficult for them to change. Sometimes demonic influence may go unnoticed if it is aimed at decision-making as it can appear to be good but is not God's best for the person. When a person tries to change a pattern of thinking that is the consequence of some trauma, the demonic realm may activate associated pain, fear, or anger in an attempt to stop the process. As a result, the person may use avoidance strategies, while reasoning that this is their way to cope. But they are not free. Jesus tells us about strongholds in our lives can hold us in bondage[107] and reveals the solution,

> *"hold to My teaching …. then you will know the truth, and the truth will set you free."* John 8:31-32

Paul confirms this and explains that this is how we will know God's will for our lives,

> *"be transformed by the renewing of your mind, so that you may prove what the will of God is, that which is good and acceptable and perfect."* Romans 12:2

As we soak in the Word of God keeping our focus on Jesus and His words of life, we will be filled with life and peace. Unless we are determined to receive and obey the wisdom of God we will be tossed back and forth like a wave of the sea.[108]

---

107 John 8:34.
108 James 1:5-8.

In James 4:7-10 we find three commands followed by the fruit of obedience. These are, *"Submit....to God"*, *"resist the devil"*, *"draw near to God"*, and *"He will draw near to you"*.

Submit to God

It is our responsibility to renew our minds with the Word of God, taking captive every thought contrary to the truth by rejecting it. We may need God's help to discern wrong thinking because we can so easily be blinded. What we perceive, feel, hear...is not always the truth even when we are convinced so within ourselves. We can only discern the truth when we come humbly before God and ask Him to reveal it. As we read the Word of God, He brings what is wrong in our lives to our attention and so we can begin to change with His help.

James 1:8 warns us against doublemindedness as a cause of instability in all our ways when he writes *"Such a person is double-minded and unstable in all they do."* At times it can seem as though we have two distinct and separated areas in our minds and switch from one to the other depending upon circumstances. We may even be blind to the fact that we are doing this. Sometimes we excuse ourselves by saying that this is just the way we are and hopelessness sets in because we feel unable to change. However, Jesus came with good news, and He is able to help us to discover who we really are and to live in the fullness of it. Through fellowship with the Holy Spirit and meditation on the word of God our harmful rigid rock-like thinking can be broken down until transformation begins to take place. The battle is finally won and maintained by choosing to believe and live in the truth and by repetition of that truth until it becomes rooted in our hearts. Without our persistence and the grace of God helping us to change we cannot be free.

If, despite doing all of this, we are sensing a relentless "driven-ness" towards our former way of thinking then there may be an evil spirit around us or within reinforcing it. We can render this ineffectual by taking the steps mentioned under the heading below, "Resist the Devil". As we determine not to give room to the lies, any evil spirit reinforcing them will know that it is defeated and will leave when commanded to do so in the name of Jesus.

Resist the devil

As we learn to think in line with God's Word any stronghold becomes progressively weaker and the influence of any evil spirit has to leave when commanded to do so in Jesus' name. Once we are living a lifestyle of actively rejecting the wrong thought, we can move in with the authority given to us in Christ to remove any evil spirit associated with the stronghold in Jesus' name.

If the thought pattern is one that we recognize in family members or previous generations then it may be one that is driven by an evil spirit that is being passed from generation to generation. In this case we can use our authority in Jesus' name to cut ourselves free from that generational spirit together with its influences and effects. It is usual to specify it, for example an evil spirit of bitterness, unforgiveness, anger, fear or jealousy. Then, in Jesus' name we can cut any ungodly soul and spirit ties we may have with those in whom we recognize the thought pattern. This was fully explained in the previous chapter. These two steps are important as they stop the generational influences and effects of an evil spirit from continuing to harass us when we are focussing on being set free. It is a good idea to pray these two steps as soon as we recognize a stronghold because the battle to transform our minds is then no longer compounded by generational influences.

Once we have taken the first two steps our battle can focus on removing the effects that any such evil spirit has on our present thinking. This third step involves a decision of the will in that we choose to align our thoughts with the word of God by repenting of and rejecting our wrong thinking with a declaration such as,

> *In Jesus' name, I reject (fill in the name). In Jesus' name I bind the evil spirit of (fill in the name), and sever it from its power and give the power to Jesus. (This reduces the power of the spirit making it easier to remove it, and also lessens the power available in the demonic realm on earth.) In Jesus' name I command the spirit of (fill in the name) to leave me and go to Jesus' feet. Lord Jesus, I ask You to close the door against this spirit, and to fill me with the Holy Spirit and help me to continue in the truth.*

As you can see, there are three parts to this prayer: the first is repentance or turning away from any wrong thinking or attitude, the second is a command in the name of Jesus ordering any associated evil spirit to leave, and the third is a prayer to Jesus to fill, strengthen and heal us through His Spirit and then choosing to believe the truth.

Draw near to God

Having taken the steps above, we remain close to God, seeking His grace in maintaining our renewed thinking until it becomes first nature. Once our behaviour and actions automatically line up with our renewed thinking it is an indication that it has become part of our subconscious thought life and has become rooted in our hearts.[109] It is a bit like the difference between driving a car when we are learning and driving it after a few years of experience.

---

109 Proverbs 4:23.

And He will draw near to you

As our souls come into agreement with our spirits, we can have heart belief about what is promised in God's word. Bringing that life of Jesus into our souls and bodies is a lifelong process, made possible through our obedience and through the grace of God. Light replaces any darkness in our souls whenever we receive truth in place of a lie, and emotional releasing and healing replaces damaged emotions and buried pain. Repentance, forgiveness, and inner healing are all part of the ongoing process. Even with all this progressively coming into place there can still be hidden attitudes and feelings that we have no explanation for other than that they are part of our fallen nature. The Psalmist writes,

> *"Search me, O God, and know my heart; try me and know my anxious thoughts; see if there is any offensive way in me (any hurtful way in me-NASB) and lead me in the way everlasting."* Psalm 139:24

Some time ago I asked God to open any door in my life (mind, emotions, will etc) that was still closed to Him. I knew that only He could see any areas or ways in which He was shut out and I didn't want Him shut out of any part of my life. I was not aware of anything specific happening that day but a couple of days later He asked me whether I could say the words, "Father, I know you love me". Although I knew the truth of these words, I found them incredibly hard to say. He indicated that they were words I needed to be able to say. I persevered trying to say them and eventually they flowed freely from deep within me to my heavenly Father. It was just after this that God showed me the picture of me as the temple in which He dwells, and He also revealed that an evil spirit of death had left at the time I had found freedom in being able to say the words directly to my Father.

This was an example of something in my life that needed changing but that I had not been aware of. The more we think in line with the truth, that is, with Jesus, the less likely it is that we are hindering Him in the flow of His presence in us and through us. Only He can bring the hidden things to light. For example, paranoia about not being liked and accepted is a false mindset that can lead to thinking and actions that are aimed at protecting us from criticism. Such thinking and consequent actions hold us prisoners to ourselves and restrict the freedom of Christ within us.

A few days after I was free in being able to declare verbally that my Father loves me, I heard Him say, "Come back to your Father" and as I sat in His presence, He led me to read,

> "I beseech you, therefore, brethren, by the mercies of God that you present your bodies as a living sacrifice, acceptable to God, which is your reasonable service. And do not be conformed to this world, but be transformed by the renewing of your mind, that you may prove what is that good and acceptable and perfect will of God." Romans 12:1-2

God is urging us to offer our bodies and souls to Him so that we may walk on God's path following the Holy Spirit and be directed into a lifestyle of worshipping and honouring God in soul and body as well as in spirit. Only as we allow ourselves to be transformed by the renewal of our minds will we know what is pleasing to God and in His perfect will. When our minds are transformed, we have life and peace as children of God,

> "For you have not received a spirit of slavery leading to fear again, but you have received a spirit of adoption as sons by which we cry out, 'Abba Father'. The Spirit Himself testifies with our spirit that we are children of God. .... also, we ourselves, having the first fruits of the Spirit, even we ourselves groan within ourselves, waiting

eagerly for our adoption as sons, the redemption of the body."
Romans 8:15-16, 23

For the present, we have the first fruits of the Spirit but we will experience the fullness of all that it means to be sons and daughters of God when we are set free from corruption in this world and are in the fullness of God's glory. As we walk in the Spirit, allowing the Spirit to lead and guide us, His life flows throughout our mortal bodies[110] and we enjoy koinonia peace, the peace that Paul urges us to nurture and that leads us into fellowship born out of shared worship of God in the Spirit,

> *"Make every effort to keep the unity of the Spirit through the bond of peace."* Ephesians 4:3

Let us pray that the Holy Spirit will expose all our false mindsets so that we may set our minds on the things of the Spirit, and present our bodies as a spiritual act of worship, knowing that we belong to Christ. We can use the apostle John's prayer that in all respects we may prosper and be in good health, just as our soul prospers.[111]

---

110 Romans 8:11.
111 3 John 1:2.

Chapter 2:4
The Realms

"For our struggle is not against flesh and Blood, but against the rulers, against the authorities, against the powers of this dark world and against the spiritual forces of evil in the heavenly places."
Ephesians 6:12

We had been ministering in Inner Healing and Deliverance for two years before God began to teach us about how the powers of this dark world organised themselves into groups with specific job functions. These He called "realms". I am well aware that there are many, many ways in which each of us is led by God in the ministry of deliverance and so I am not suggesting that what follows is the only way. It is the way that we were taught and that works for us. Over the years I have ministered alongside others who have different approaches, but it has never been a problem as we all have the one goal, that of working together under God for the releasing of those under bondage. Within the context of ministry, we have found these insights invaluable and have used them to lead many into freedom.

A "realm" is "a royal domain". A realm implies the authority of a ruler over its domain, the scope of its activity, perhaps with specific characteristics. God gave us the names of eight realms, each with four subcategories forming a demonic stronghold. Through seeing each of the realms in action over a period of thirty years we have come to understand some of the characteristics of each and how they affect people. Consequently, under the leading of the Holy Spirit, we have been shown how to pray relevantly in order to achieve freedom, primarily with people but, also, for our church (which is a group of people), for our town, and for our country and the nations.

The eight realms are Antichrist, Lucifer, Ahab, Jezebel, Witchcraft, Idolatry, Death and Hell and Deception. Each of these is a family or cluster of four, each of which is like a wall and, together, form a demonic stronghold. A selection of some of the characteristics are,

- Antichrist: rape, distortion, mimicry, genocide

- Lucifer: pride, legalism, chaos, confusion

- Ahab: lethargy, hatred, apathy, fear

- Jezebel: seductiveness, control, conniving, flattery

- Witchcraft: rebellion, control, mockery, sickness

- Idolatry: fornication, arrogance, backbiting, jealousy

- Death and Hell: division, discouragement, dissension, destruction

- Deception: falsehood, hypocrisy, good works, false worship or teaching of the Word

Each of the realms represents aspects of satan. The realm of Lucifer is not Lucifer in the sense of being satan as such, but includes many of his characteristics, some of which are described in Ezekiel 28. A person can be affected by the realm of witchcraft without being a participant in the craft. This will all become clear as we explore the characteristics of the different realms in the following chapters.

Some further insights

1. Demonic or evil spirits are the lowest in the hierarchy of spirits and are confined to harassing individuals.

2. A stronghold comes about through wrong thinking, beliefs or attitudes in a specific area. If a person persistently sins in that area an evil spirit may take advantage, gaining entry and consequently enforcing that behaviour. It then becomes difficult for the person to change unless they remove the offending spirit in Jesus' name. A stronghold can be developed amongst a group of people, e.g., a church. In a stronghold there are different levels of governing, the one at the top being called the strongman.

3. Deliverance of people from evil spirits lessons the power of the stronghold.

4. Pulling down the stronghold in an area lessens the pressured effect of that stronghold on people. If the demonic is bound it allows the people to recognise their sin and have space to repent and be cleansed.

5. The classification of strongholds, ruling spirits etc. in job function, is fairly arbitrary because each can imitate anything lower down the hierarchy and can enlist the help of others. For example, the realm of Witchcraft may join with the realm of Ahab at times for a particular task, each fulfilling its role.

6. In addition to these eight realms, we came to learn later about Beelzebub, the most powerful evil spirit of all, and as near to satan as an evil spirit can be. Beelzebub can be any of the realms whenever he so chooses. He has a particular role in replacing a person's lost identity with a false one. This will be explained in the Book 3 chapter 2.2.

7. Each of the realms has some characteristics in common with other realms but each is distinctive when observed through

an awareness of how they function. Each has a different focus on how they cause division, disruption, antagonism and separateness from God, but they have a common goal, to go against Jesus by alienating His people. Dependence on the Holy Spirit to give insight is crucial.

8. It is clear that satan uses many realms and evil spirits in his battle against God's Kingdom, and that each of these spirits want power for themselves and will only cooperate with other evil spirits if it is in their own interests. The enemy's goal is to divide and conquer in contrast to God's desire that we live in unity. Whereas satan wants division within people and amongst people, Jesus seeks to bring all people into the one Kingdom through the one Spirit as sons and daughters of God, brothers and sisters in Christ. The evil world seeks to dominate, intimidate and rule over people. Jesus came as a humble servant and invites us into His Kingdom of joy and peace through His unconditional love and mercy. Everything satan offers comes at a cost to us but everything Jesus offers is a free gift of grace. Even with all his scheming and strategies satan cannot match the power of the one true King, Jesus, nor of His heavenly realm. This is worth pausing to consider because in doing so we are built up in our faith in Jesus, and in the knowledge of the enormous victory we already have in Christ Jesus over evil. We have nothing to fear. Remember this. There is no power higher than the name of Jesus.

Chapter 2:5
The Realm of Antichrist

"Little children, it is the last time: and as ye have heard
that antichrist shall come, even now are there many antichrists; whereby
we know that it is the last time."
1 John 2:18

The Realm of Antichrist comprises spirits who are anti-Christ, anti-love, anti-forgiveness, anti-reconciliation, in fact anti anything that is Godly. They are rebellious, lawless spirits, hating authority. Through deception they portray lawlessness as liberty. They aim to bring double standards into homes and into the Church. They have a war mentality, intensely battling against the person in whom they have gained entrance, and causing disruption around them. They bring confusion, hopelessness and despair. People who have inherited and are strongly affected by such a spirit may be sadistic, enjoying inflicting pain on their family and others whether physical, mental, emotional, psychological, sexual or spiritual. This is rape. The four clusters of spirits within the stronghold of antichrist are rape, distortion, mimicry and genocide.

Spirits of antichrist have within their hierarchy spirits of selfish ambition, unbelief, rejection, rebellion, lying, anger, hatred, strife, murder, abortion, unforgiveness, bitterness, corrupt communications such as blasphemy, curses, filthy language, torment. Once recognised as the driving force behind a person's behaviour and their traits rejected as a lifestyle any evil spirit has to leave when commanded to do so in Jesus' name. Many evil spirits can be a root cause for various kinds of infirmity and, if not noticed, can hinder healing.

An antichrist spirit may make threats that are potentially disturbing but we remember that Jesus is Lord of all and protects us. On one occasion while I was ministering to someone, an antichrist spirit which could not bear to be restricted by a child of God made threats, boasting that it would kill my children. I immediately felt the strength and conviction of God's protection in my spirit and responded by quietly reminding it who I was in Christ and that my children were being kept safe. I was not phased at all by the threat and this only annoyed it even more. When it was commanded to leave in the name of Jesus, it declared haughtily that it was bored with my company and was choosing to go.

An antichrist spirit can be present in a person through heresy, through membership of a cult, or through generational iniquity. They may achieve entry through a pattern of sin sometimes borne out of a felt need or response to hurt inflicted by another. Frequently, they have been passed down through several generations. The family members with this spirit are so familiar with it that they may not question their behaviour unless convicted to do so by the Holy Spirit.

A person with an antichrist spirit can themselves feel raped, mentally, emotionally and psychologically and not realise why. They can be full of negativity, worry and fear. They can be misled about Jesus and His love for them because the spirit is feeding in its lies. Such a person can feel worthless, insecure, and not accepted, and may develop tactics to ensure that they are always seen as gracious and acceptable to others. Generally, only some characteristics of the spirit will be to the fore, but these may have become a way of life so much so that the person with such a spirit believes they are their own personality traits.

A person influenced by an antichrist spirit may believe that they are always right. What can appear as graciousness may be hiding careful psychological strategies to manipulate. Their voice can be seductive and their smile charming and strangely commanding so that they are able to draw people to them. They can be shrewd, smooth talking and flattering. Their eyes are intense and focused and communicate with what appears to be deep sincerity but they are untrustworthy. They may push for quick agreements before the other person has time to consider for themselves or they may appear to act selflessly by offering the other freedom to decide but doing so in such a way that makes their preference known, all the time asking permission, but not taking kindly to refusal. They choose words carefully and watch reactions closely, gauging body language so as to assess whether to proceed as they are doing or vary their approach. They move closer to a person, thus attempting to draw them into agreement. Little by little they take back any ground until they get exactly what they want and the other person is left wondering what happened. If thwarted, they change demeanour and inner rage replaces the sweet smooth flattery. At such times others can feel terrified by their behaviour, but it is in reality the demonic drive behind the person's behaviour that is intimidating.

If the decision is one that the person with the antichrist spirit knows they cannot change then they rehearse it in their mind, adjusting to it until it becomes their own decision and can be portrayed to other people as theirs. This then puts that person back in charge once again. They are subversive and always ensure they are in control. On the surface, the person with this spirit orchestrates apparently good things but is frequently scheming and plotting to their own ends. Those on the receiving end gradually realise something is wrong but find it difficult to fault the actions of the other and so end up blaming themselves for being unreasonable. Such a person loses peace and lives with confusion and a dislike of themselves because of how they are feeling.

Since "self" is at the centre, a person with an antichrist spirit will project themselves as considerate of others while at the same time possibly harbouring wrong attitudes like jealousy. If they become aware of jealousy within, they may move into denial so as to avoid dealing with the issue. Unfortunately, this does not resolve such issues and leads to inner torment for the person. Continuing divided attitudes of mind and heart within them can cause cursing of the object of their jealousy. Such a curse can debilitate a person, sucking the life out of them, and create a barrier so that they have difficulty in communicating and thinking logically. Their freedom is severely curtailed, perhaps stopped, and immobilisation occurs.

From the above discussion it can be seen that a strategy of antichrist spirits is to mesmerise and immobilise.

Some symptoms felt by a person who is being subjected to the presence of this evil spirit in another are pressure in the head, inability to remember things, loss of visionary capacity, and a realisation that that they are being manipulated into changing their decisions without being able to understand how it happens. There can be an awareness of a strong "magnetic" effect towards the person while in their presence but not when absent from them. They may have a sense of going round in circles and not moving forward with God, and experience a loss of interest in participating in spiritual things although still having a desire to be close to God and hear His direction. If anyone stands against this antichrist type behaviour in a person, they likely will receive an onslaught of accusation accompanied by intimidation. They have a sense of powerlessness to change things because of inability to see what is wrong.

The person influenced by this evil spirit may behave this way in order to avoid rejection and confrontation from others but, as a consequence, they cause hurt, division and confusion, "*A house divided cannot stand*" Mark 3:25. Generally, they are completely unaware that they cause disruption. They can have a serious effect on the body of Christ if allowed to continue undetected. Anyone with an antichrist spirit has responsibility to change from a lifestyle of control and manipulation to one of submission to God.

A person affected by another with an antichrist spirit will probably lose their peace and not understand why because the deviousness of this spirit makes it difficult to discern. Thankfully this loss of peace is a warning sign and a signal to spend time with God finding out the reason,

> "*The peace that Christ gives is to guide you in the decisions you make; for it is to this peace that God has called you together in the one body. And be thankful*". Colossians 3:15

I have come to the realisation that when God is teaching me something new about how evil spirits can harass people, He doesn't give me a solution quickly as He wants me to experience and really understand the distress caused by such spirits. Little by little He gives me insight and confirmations until I am equipped to resolve anything that such a spirit can inflict on a person. For me these lessons were learnt the hard way, but I pray the insights that follow will equip you to recognise antichrist deception quickly.

On one occasion I struggled for six months against many of the symptoms that I have just described before God told me that I was being bewitched by a certain person. One definition indicates that this is the ability, *"to attract or interest someone a lot so that you have the power to influence them" and "to put a magic spell on someone or something in order to control him, her, or it."*[112]

Shortly after this, a word, "trans-liminal" (not "subliminal") surfaced from within my spirit, a word which is not in the dictionary and which I had never come across. It seemed that I was being led to understand that thoughts, attitudes, desires were being transferred from the evil spirit "across" to me in such a way as to influence my own thoughts without my being aware. "Trans-limination" works on the mind and emotions but, thank God, it cannot affect the spirit of those who have the Holy Spirit. The evidence of "trans-limination" is elusive and only truly recognised when God steps in with His protection against it and reveals it for what it is.

During this process of discovery, I awoke one morning with the thought, "counsel of the wicked" and immediately recalled the scripture,

"Blessed is the one who does not walk in step with the wicked or stand in the way that sinners take or sit in the company of mockers." Psalm 1:1

Another morning I awoke with the thought, "trapped". This was exactly how I had been feeling. Little by little, the Holy Spirit within was giving me revelation so as to guide me towards freedom. That freedom finally came through God giving me prayers that would protect my mind and so free it from the influences and effects of this antichrist spirit. I was to put on the armour of God,[113] protect my mind through applying the Blood of Jesus over the threshold of my mind at all three levels, conscious, subconscious and unconscious, and I was to place the cross of Jesus between me and the antichrist

---

112 Cambridge English Dictionary.
113 Ephesians 6:10-18.

spirit (evil spirits don't like to be reminded of their defeat at the cross). A friend summarised it as the ABC of protection. I was also told to pray for a wall of flame around me. From this time on, I was able to discern every move of the antichrist spirit working through the person. The difference for me was immediate and totally releasing, and I began to experience peace again. How wonderful it is to have God's protection against these evil powers.

From that point on I was given many confirmations that it had been an antichrist spirit that had targeted me, and was given further insight about its character through the name, "Robespierre", coming to mind. I did not know who this was and so looked up Wikipedia[114] where I found an interesting article about this well-known, influential figure in the French Revolution. These few excerpts witnessed to me that God was affirming the targeting of an antichrist spirit against me. I have italicized these,

> Robespierre's speeches were exceptional, and *he had the power to change the views of almost any audience.* His speaking techniques included *invocation of virtue and morals,* and quite often the use of rhetorical questions in order to *identify with the audience.* He would gesticulate and use ideas and personal experiences in life to keep listeners' attentions. His final method was to state that *he was always prepared to die in order to save the Revolution.[115]*

> Because he believed that the Revolution was still in progress, and in danger of being sabotaged, he made every attempt to instil in the populace and Convention the urgency of carrying out the Terror. *Robespierre saw no room for mercy in his Terror,* stating that *"slowness of judgments is equal to impunity"* and *"uncertainty of punishment encourages all the guilty".[116]*

---

114 https://www.academia.edu/17843956/Maximilien_Robespierre_Wikipedia_the_free_encyclopedia
115 Schama 1989, p. 579.
116 Gordon Kerr. Leaders Who Changed the World. Canary Press. p. 17.

It is not violent fulminations that characterise Robespierre's speeches on the Terror. It is *the language* of unmasking, unveiling, revealing, discovering, *exposing the enemy within*, the enemy hidden behind patriotic posturings, the language of suspicion.[117]

Shortly after this, the word, "Platypus" rose up from my spirit. Again, I researched the word in Wikipedia,

the spurs on the male's back ankles deliver venom, ... unique to the platypus. .... in platypuses they also are formed into *venom for defence*. Although powerful enough to kill smaller animals such as dogs, the venom is not lethal to humans, but the pain is so excruciating that *the victim may be incapacitated.*[118]

As final confirmation, the words, "Venus flytrap" were brought to me by a friend. The Venus Flytrap waits, checks its victim as edible and then closes its "jaws" around unsuspecting insects. That described how I had felt. God gave me insight that this antichrist spirit had been targeting me to take me off course from God's plan for my life. God will not be thwarted in such a way.

One day shortly after I had gained freedom from its influence, I was reminded of a scripture given to me thirty years previously,

"but the people that do know their God shall be strong and do exploits." Daniel 11: 32 KJV

This reminder strengthened me once again in my recently found freedom. In the New International Version, this same verse reads,

---

117 Doyle, Robespierre. 1999. Page 27.
118 https://en.wikipedia.org/wiki/Platypus

*"but the people who know their God will firmly resist
him".* Daniel 11:32

The context suggests that this resistance is against "he who corrupts
with flattery". I was amused at this because it confirmed yet again
what I had been up against. Once again, I was able to hear God's voice
readily and, while in my room at home, heard the words, "Prayer
Haven" and "lo, the winter is over. Now, you're on the right road, the
one God planned for you".

It is important to ask God for understanding and revelation as to
how He sees a person with an antichrist spirit because then we can
sense God's compassion and mercy for the person, and pray for them
with His heart. Any battle we have is really with the enemy and
not with people.

Some years later, whenever I was in ministry with a particular person,
I would feel my chest being crushed very heavily so much so that I
could hardly breathe. It felt as though something was mimicking a
heart attack. However, some weeks earlier God had told me that He
had given me the gift of "Divine Health", and as I declared this truth
the crushing slowly left. As I puzzled over this, I awoke one morning
with the words, "1793 battle", in my mind. When I researched this,
I found that this was the time of the rise of Robespierre for his one
year "reign of terror". This was confirmation that an antichrist spirit
was working against me and so it was duly dispatched in Jesus' name
during the following session of ministry.

Examples of people with an antichrist spirit in scripture are Haman
in the book of Esther, and those who opposed the building of the
wall in the time of Nehemiah. This spirit's main goal is that in men's
eyes Jesus is seen as dead or irrelevant, but the good news is that all
evil spirits have already been defeated at the cross and we only have to
enforce that victory in Jesus,

"for everyone born of God overcomes the world. This is the victory that has overcome the world, even our faith. Who is it that overcomes the world? Only the one who believes that Jesus is the Son of God." 1 John 5:4-5

To become free from the effects and influences of an antichrist spirit in another person, it is necessary to ignore feelings and focus on Jesus while using the ABC prayers of protection. If we have this spirit affecting us from within, we can seek God's help to discern any ungodly behaviour and choose to change. Then we can command the spirit to leave in Jesus' name and ask Him to fill those areas which have been vacated with His Holy Spirit and close any door that would allow re-entry. This enables us to regain freedom and be at peace. If we abide in Jesus we can pray, "Thy will be done" (which infers our obedience to His will) and "lead us not into temptation but deliver us from evil", knowing that He will intercept satan in his attempts at influencing us and help us to stand firm. This includes attempts from any spirit of antichrist to put thoughts into our minds.

It is extremely important for us as Christians to exercise discernment by being actively alert to it within our spirits. When we feel peace, all is well. When we feel unrest, irritation, heaviness etc. then we need to heed the warning and ask God for revelation. With discernment we can know whether something being taught is truth according to scripture and in keeping with God's character. We can discern when an evil spirit is adversely affecting ourselves or someone else and what that spirit is. When, as an adult, I asked Jesus to give me discernment, He told me that I already had it but that He had put a veil over it when I was a baby to protect me from excessive terror. I asked Him to take this off. I then had two dreams which gave me understanding as to why God had put a veil over my discernment and why I had a suffered such terror so consistently throughout my life when in the presence of those in authority.

In one of the dreams, I was shown myself as a baby in the house where I had grown up and it was clear to me that at that time, I had sensed an evil spirit touching me in the back of my neck. I cried and cried in absolute terror. When I awoke God revealed to me that when I was a year old, I had discerned in my spirit that something evil was near me. It had been an antichrist spirit and, because of my Godly heritage, God had put the veil in place over my discernment as a form of protection while I was growing up. I was given insight that the antichrist spirit had been attempting to frighten me so that I would never stand against such spirits. As I reflected afterwards on the people who had intimidated and terrified me throughout my life, I recognized the work of an antichrist spirit through many of them.

What I have written about antichrist spirits and their influences and effects is not intended as an exhaustive (and exhausting!) overview. I have chosen to give you these insights into my experience with antichrist spirits so that you may be equipped to stand against them. What is really exciting for us all is the consistency with which they, having already been defeated at the cross, are evicted in Jesus' name from the lives of those that they torment, and are prevented from harassing others. All thankfulness and glory belong to God!

Chapter 2:6
The Realm of Lucifer

".... your heart is lifted up, and you say, 'I am a god, I sit in the seat of gods, in the midst of the seas....'"
Ezekiel 28:2

The Realm of Lucifer is not limited to the fallen archangel Lucifer (now named satan), but includes those spirits that are most like it in character. It is extremely powerful in satan's kingdom. Lucifer spirits are connected ultimately with death and will often work with the spirit of death but they will use any of the realms to work alongside them for their own gain, protecting them only when it suits. The four clusters of spirits within a stronghold of Lucifer are pride, legalism, chaos and confusion.

Lucifer spirits can be present by virtue of legal ground given by ancestors or by ourselves. They magnify existing pain, pressure and hurt where given an opportunity. This is one reason why it is important to talk to God, repenting of sin, forgiving others, and resolving issues as we journey through life. Prolonged emotional upheaval, wrong attitudes such as unforgiveness, pride, self-seeking, ambition, legalism or religiosity and not resolving ongoing pressures and stresses make us vulnerable to these spirits.

Lucifer spirits aim to focus worship leaders and fellow worshippers alike on emotions alone, thus directing worship away from Jesus. Consequently, emotional hype may be mistaken for true worship. A worship leader who deliberately moves with a Lucifer spirit in targeting the emotions of others so as to produce hype is serving their own needs.

Conversely, a godly worship leader may have a battle trying to break through into pure worship of Jesus where there is lack of spiritual engagement by the congregation. Even when a spirit of Lucifer is present, those who are truly worshipping Jesus in their hearts will push through into a connection with God.

It is incumbent upon all to seek to worship God in *spirit and in truth*.[119] True worship of Jesus flows where there is unity of focus and purpose, not only in our minds, emotions, hearts, and bodies, but in our spirits also. Our spirits become alive with the profound reality of the worth of God and a desire to honour Him above all. True worship of Jesus encourages others to worship in spirit and truth also.

When leaders preach the Word of God under the leading of the Holy Spirit people sense the presence of Jesus and respond with faith and hope and with a desire to please God through obedience and change. Lucifer spirits want to stop all of this from happening and so will try by any means to hinder God's servant from proclaiming God's word, perhaps by causing situations that divert them from preparation or by distracting them while speaking. He is not short of ideas. Where a person is not walking humbly with God and giving God the glory at all times they may unintentionally collude with the Lucifer spirit in seeking to get attention on self and get the glory that should go to God. If this is so then the teaching may be correct, but it will bring death, condemnation, accusation, and heaviness. This is the

---

119 John 4:23.

religious aspect of a Lucifer spirit affecting the speaker. On the other hand, where the Spirit is there is life, light, encouragement and focus on Jesus. When praying for our pastors and worship leaders, and for the congregation, we can pray prayers that stop Lucifer spirits from interfering. He is full of pride[120] and so the best antidote to a Lucifer spirit is,

> *"to walk humbly with God and to act justly and to love mercy."*
> Micah 6:8

In the body of Christ Lucifer spirits target faith-filled, charismatic and evangelical gatherings and may infiltrate leadership in support ministries, fostering pride, divisiveness and rebelliousness. They use illegitimate authority, stealing the hearts of people.

A person with a Lucifer spirit can be so influenced by it when coming to faith that they may be prevented from entering into the freedom of the Holy Spirit and a true relationship with Jesus. They may find it difficult to pray and read scripture. Sometimes, they may appear to be very spiritual, having a self-righteous front and zealous to a fault in demonstrating godliness, but it's superficial and not from their heart. A person influenced by this spirit may be hard-hearted, unforgiving, aggressive and condemnatory, judgmental and unmerciful, and burden others. They may focus on duty rather than love, know all the answers scripturally and enjoy airing their knowledge. Paul in writing to the Corinthian church warned them about this with these words,

> *"Knowledge makes arrogant, but love edifies."* 1 Corinthians 8:1

The outward form of religion may deceive others but discernment will reveal self-centredness, self-interest, ambition and a lack of the

---

120 Isaiah 14:12-15.

fruit of the Holy Spirit. Those with the gentle Spirit of God teach in humility, thereby bringing freedom.[121]

Spirits of Lucifer are rebellious, stirring up chaos and causing confusion. A person with a Lucifer spirit may be totally unable to bring order to anything, and may cause havoc wherever they go. Chaos within a church setting can distract Church leaders away from what is important onto resolving peripheral issues. Evil spirits can only use people to suit their purposes if they allow it through refusing to change un-Godly behaviour with God's help.

Lucifer spirits, like Antichrist and Ahab spirits, can put accusing and condemning thoughts into people's minds. They may cause division in families, churches, businesses etc., while blaming others. Where present in a church meeting, they may direct those present towards decisions that are not God's choice at that moment.

Lucifer spirits use all three aspects of witchcraft: manipulation, domination and intimidation. They provoke rebellion, accusation, manipulation, control, lying, anger, arrogance, super-spirituality, rumour-spreading, criticism, jealousy, craftiness, false concern. If a person is being affected by the Lucifer spirit it is more than likely that only one or two aspects of the spirit are noticeably present but, nevertheless, it can have a devastating effect, especially on a person's freedom in Christ.

Lucifer spirits present within a person may cause internal friction which, in turn, can lead to the person's own body fighting against itself and causing a breakdown in the immune system with consequent infection. In one person, who had been diagnosed with fibromyalgia, a generational spirit of Lucifer over her spirit and in her soul was commanded to go in Jesus' name and then we asked God to heal her

---

121 Micah 6:8.

from the effects and influences. The symptoms of the fibromyalgia completely left. Not all sicknesses are caused by evil spirits but those that are can be removed by expelling the spirits responsible and asking God to heal the person from any effects and influences. Some evil spirits collude causing all sorts of health problems so we need to seek Jesus as the way forward to freedom will vary. Witchcraft spirits outside a person can imitate symptoms and try to make the person believe that they have a particular illness such as arthritis. If the person believes the symptoms this gives a right of entry for the associated spirit. The person will then be affected more and more by the symptoms of arthritis.[122]

Clearly, our battle is against the spiritual forces of evil in the heavenly realms.[123] Sadly, we may allow ourselves to co-operate with the ungodly ways of evil. The more we walk in the Spirit the less these evil spirits can use us in their obstructive and destructive work and so be starved of power until, eventually, they have to go even if they have not already been ordered out. Particularly sad is the fact that some will use these spirits to further their own cause. The instruction in Micah 6:8 is important if we want to walk with God and be free from the effects and influences of these evil powers.

The discernment of the Spirit of God enables us to detect Lucifer's presence and influence. We can pray for protection for ourselves and for all our leaders as they take their places in the public arena.

It is important for us all to be listening to the Spirit of God consistently so that we are not ignorant of the enemy's schemes but can thwart him,

"Be alert and of sober mind. Your enemy the devil prowls around like a roaring lion looking for someone to devour. Resist him,

---

122 Book 2, chapter 5:9.
123 Ephesians 6:12.

standing firm in the faith, because you know that the family of believers throughout the world is undergoing the same kind of sufferings." 1 Peter 5:8-9

Chapter 2:7

The Realm of Ahab

In the hierarchy of evil spirits, the Realm of Ahab spirits is next in authority to that of Lucifer spirits. However, they serve Lucifer spirits only when it suits and will not serve any other spirit as they think of themselves as more important. In the demonic realm they have the authority of kings. The Ahab spirit takes its name from King Ahab of Israel, "the troubler of Israel."[124] The characteristics that we see played out in King Ahab's life demonstrate some of the characteristics of Ahab spirits. The four clusters of spirits within the stronghold of Ahab are lethargy, hatred (sectarianism), fear (doubt, insecurity, sensitivity) and apathy.

When a person consistently worships something or someone other than God this can give a foothold for an evil Ahab spirit. A recommitment and affirmation of worship of God weakens it.

---

124 1 Kings 18:17.

Many who inherit an Ahab spirit from a previous generation are completely unaware of its existence let alone its presence within them, believing that any characteristics and thoughts that actually come from an Ahab spirit are their own. In observing how their predecessors dealt with adverse situations they may have learned to use similar methods and so be living in collusion with the spirit without realising it. However, once they understand what is happening, and come out of agreement with the spirit's characteristics, Jesus will remove it.

Those behaving with characteristics of an Ahab spirit usually portray themselves as "Mr Nice Guy" (or "Ms"), are generally outwardly gracious in demeanour and well-liked by those around them, never appearing to do any wrong. They can be extremely strong willed and stubborn but with a pleasant veneer. However, they scheme, cajole and plan using deceitful methods so as to get their own way. They manipulate others into feeling sorry for them or inspire fear using furtive methods. They frequently have difficulty in their relationships, for example, a person with an Ahab character can control their spouse in a gathering with a look or with a gesture, while at the same time being the life and soul of the party.

Where someone is moving with the spirit's characteristics it will appear to others that they are able to get their own way without offence and yet it's not obvious how. This is because their control has a "kid glove" or "under the counter" approach, not easily recognised by others because it is covert. They like to have people around them with strong Jezebel spirits because such people will do or get for them what they want and since their control is easily recognised, they will be seen as responsible for any fall-out (cf. King Ahab and Queen Jezebel). Anyone who feels controlled and manipulated by a person with this spirit can rarely point to a specific example and any attempts to do so often appear to be petty and insignificant and others observing usually don't recognise Ahab behaviour in action. Since the person with this spirit doesn't like confrontation, they make it appear as though the person on the receiving end is being unreasonable and so that person's sense of being trapped can intensify. Discernment from God is needed to recognise this spirit at work within a person.

Sadly, a person with an Ahab spirit often manipulates and controls in this way because they themselves are fearful and lacking in confidence in their own identity and beliefs. As is usually true in his destructive work of causing division and destruction, satan seeks to destroy both the one with an evil spirit as well as those around them. Jesus seeks the opposite. He loves each, and in His mercy and grace, will reach out to heal and free both. As His children, this is how we are to relate to one another as well. Many of those victimising others have been or are victims as well and need understanding and grace. Jesus is gentle and kind with everyone, while maintaining righteousness and truth.

The Ahab spirit has many characteristics, which, when put together, define it but nobody with an Ahab spirit will move in all the characteristics. When God was teaching us about this spirit He called it the "octopus spirit" because, like an octopus, it has lots of arms (tentacles) in its arsenal. What I describe now are some of the characteristics of Ahab spirits that we have experienced within the context of ministry,

- They are angry, resentful — 1 Kings 19; 21: 4.

- They are idolatrous — 1 Kings 16: 29ff; 21;26.

- They are people pleasers — 1 Kings 20: 3,4,7.

- They are adept at using subterfuge — 1 Kings 22: 30.

- They are fearful of confrontation.

- They are manipulators and controllers.

- They taunt.

- They are murderers.

- They are selfish and covetous.

- They are jealous.

- They are cowardly.

- They are liars and deceivers.

- They display self-pity and are sympathy seekers — 1 Kings 19:1-2. They can focus a person on their lack and away from what is good, nurturing self-pity.

- They allow those who fight on their behalf to do so under their authority. King Ahab let Jezebel use his seals — 1 Kings 21:8.

- They are persistent and persevere rather than admit defeat.

- They are of evil intent and sold out to evil — 1Kings 21:20.

- They have contempt for God's prophets — 1Kings 22:8.

- They are able to project their thinking onto a person whether from outside the person of from within by using words like, "I" and "my".

- They make a person feel worthless.

- They can cut off a person from their emotions.

- They can block a person's memory.

- They can block a person's cognitive abilities and focus by causing fogginess, blurred vision, confusion and doubt and dull awareness.

- They can block out God's voice by putting their suggestion forward, enticing people into thinking that they are hearing the voice of the Holy Spirit when they are not.

- They are able to imitate trance by inducing a trance-like state to suit their purposes or to divert attention from themselves.

- They can imitate paralysis.

- They can cause tiredness/weariness/lethargy.

- They can cause agitation physically, sometimes restless legs.

- They may be responsible for affecting appetite.

- They are observant.

- They are stirrers and troublemakers.

- They can have a powerful underhand attraction when they choose and may draw people into sexual immorality.

- They like being dominated sexually but do not like being controlled.

- They are masters at distraction.

- They distort communication amongst people.

- They are able to use other people to do their talking for them through controlling their thinking.

It is evident that Ahab evil spirits are friends with no-one. They back-stab, fuel accusations, issue comments with condemnation implied and distract people from keeping appointments. When we are helping a person to get free from this spirit, we may need to remove its hold in each area bit by bit, thus weakening the spirit before completing the removal.

One of the serious aspects of an Ahab spirit is their interference when a person wants to hear God. We can prevent this obstruction by binding and commanding it not to interfere or communicate in the name of Jesus. Even after taking such precautions, we need to check everything that prompts us into action so that we discern the source correctly. Ahab spirits may pre-empt what God is doing in that they may give earlier timing and so lead a person into something at a time when there may be danger at worst, and lack of fruit at best.

On one occasion when I was leading a seminar, I was unable to speak with freedom, and it felt as though the participants in the seminar were in chains because of the presence of an Ahab spirit. I asked God to send fiery angels into the seminar room to stop the Ahab spirit from affecting us all (Ahab spirits hate fire). The difference was immediate. I no longer felt any interference and the people became relaxed and chatty. The only other spirit that can act exactly like an Ahab spirit is a spirit of deception which can copy this demonic or, indeed, any other evil spirit apart from Jezebel and Lucifer spirits that wouldn't allow themselves to be so used. Sometimes evil spirits work together when it suits them, for example, one time an Ahab spirit and a spirit of deception worked together with the spirit of deception masquerading as an Ahab spirit. This made it appear that there was a double layer of Ahab spirits so that when one was removed there still appeared to be another. If God had not revealed that one was deception, we may have mistakenly tried to remove a second Ahab spirit.

An example of how an Ahab spirit in one person can affect another member of the family became evident in a family where the father was alcoholic and abused his wife. The Ahab spirit in the father had settled as an imprint over the daughter who had been terrified of his outbursts. This all-embracing imprint over the daughter had plagued her with irrational fears and terrors over the years. It was also affecting her spouse. Once the imprint was gone, the fears left the wife and the husband was no longer affected.

An Ahab spirit within a person can use a person for its own ends and, if desired, link up with Ahab spirits in other people. What appears as confirmation of a fact through others may only be the spirit Ahab putting its thoughts into different people's minds so that they confirm something as true. This can also happen when this evil spirit is outside each person and putting thoughts their way. An extreme use of Ahab in this way would be to influence decisions being made in an important meeting. Such use of Ahab can be stopped by severing between the Ahab spirits and commanding them not to communicate in Jesus' name and then severing each person attending the meeting from any Ahab spirit together with its influences and effects in Jesus' name. It is wise to take these precautions before meetings so that all participants are free to express their own views.

If a person has something like a skin of Ahab, then that person needs to step out of the skin in Jesus' name. Some effects of a skin of Ahab are sudden tiredness, loss of memory and concentration, fear and anxiety over inconsequential things or irrational worries. Sometimes it takes the form of obsessional behaviour such as continually checking whether electricity is turned off and never being confident that it is. It may affect the person with low self-esteem.

As I have already mentioned, it is completely wrong for us to minister throughout the process of deliverance as if we are doing something for the person. It is really helpful to the person to know that they are contributing to their own freedom and, as they themselves keep control of the process under God, they are encouraged to feel empowered and of value, while being discipled. Such an approach guards against the person feeling that we are addressing them if, in fact, we are addressing an evil spirit. As with all other demonic, if the person is living his life in such a way as to starve any Ahab spirit, then, sooner rather than later, it is forced into going.

Discussion can help a person struggling under the influence of an Ahab spirit to separate out their own feelings from those of the spirit so that they can discern in what way it is affecting them. Once the person knows this then they can start to work against its influence.

When an Ahab spirit surfaces in one of its many guises, we take control in Jesus' name and do not let it off with thinking that it is king with authority. It hates the mention of fire and so, if it is being a nuisance and protracting ministry, we can bind it, command it not to interfere or communicate, and threaten it with the fire of God.[125] At all times we seek to be led by Jesus in these matters. He may instruct us to put a hedge of fire around an Ahab spirit, or put it in a cylinder or some such instruction. No matter how ridiculous an instruction from God may seem to us, obedience to that instruction moves ministry forward.

Once we know that a person has an Ahab spirit (which may be dormant) we can ask God to stir up the spirit and bring it to the surface. Their motto is, "Catch me if you can!" and since they like to have the upper hand they will distract so as not to be found. For example, if an Ahab spirit thinks it is about to be uncovered, it may put the person into a trance so that they cannot respond, impose lethargy so that they have to fight to stay awake, or paralyse so that they are unable to move. As each of these distractions is caused by a spirit under Ahab's control, we can stop the distractions by binding them and commanding them not to interfere in Jesus' name. This leads to the Ahab spirit surfacing to see what's going on, and by acting quickly we can trap it by asking Jesus to stop it from hiding again. This makes it angry and exposes it for what it is - weak and not in control.

As with all spirits, Ahab spirits can link into negative emotions, often because they are initiators of them. For example, one lady who had great fear and was terrified of all men came for ministry. We asked God to break the link between the spirit of Ahab and her emotions, and then asked Him to bring up the memory that had led to the fear. After some gentle inner healing and deliverance, the

---

125 1 Kings 21:19; 22:38

fear left. If there are several Ahab spirits affecting a person then we sever between each Ahab spirit together with their influences and effects, and bind each in Jesus' name before removing them in Jesus' name, one at a time.

When a person chooses to change from ungodly mindsets and attitudes any foothold that an evil spirit has used in the past is removed and the spirit eventually leaves. As an alternative approach, the evil spirit can be commanded to leave in Jesus' name as soon as the person chooses to change as necessary. Being forced to obey because of our authority in Jesus demonstrates to evil spirits that, in Christ, we are in control and so they obey. Sometimes when an evil spirit is using delaying tactics God may send an angel to remove it. If we try to remove any evil spirit before the foothold is removed it may hide and give the impression it has gone, or go only to return with reinforcements making things worse for the person. It is best to follow God's leading.

After deliverance there is usually a noticeable joy and freedom from whatever symptoms Ahab had put on the person. It can be true, however, that once an Ahab spirit is removed, the person feels lost and without purpose, aimless and listless because they have been used to being controlled. It is important, therefore, to prepare the person before the spirit is removed so that they do not become disconcerted but understand that there will be a period of adjustment during which Jesus will strengthen and help them.

If, after deliverance, a person continues to experience the ill-effects of an Ahab spirit it may be a sign that an Ahab spirit is around but outside them. They must learn to stand against this and be strong in what they believe. A spirit of Ahab around a deaf girl who was being healed by God was hindering the process of healing but once God removed this influence, she received her hearing in full. What God does cannot be undone.

If present within a Church an Ahab spirit can affect the members, causing them to feel tired and lethargic. This is not physical tiredness which can be shaken off but a spiritual tiredness which saps us of all strength, causing us to feel helpless. It debilitates people by making them feel drained, washed out and condemned. When people are so affected others may say the right things but they may feel condemnation and be upset, and because they feel miserable want to withdraw. This is usually the result of a curse of an Ahab spirit. Once it is recognised the people can be severed from its effects and influences and restored to freedom. The difference is immediate.

If a leader with an Ahab spirit allows anyone with a Jezebel spirit to have their way with them e.g., controlling them into agreeing with their preferences and even facilitating their rise to positions of leadership then that person gives a foothold that allows the spirit of Ahab to operate round them and influence them. This can bring confusion and depression, perhaps the raising of issues without answers, and has the effect of enticing people to want their own way.

Ahab spirits are ready to jump in at any opportunity and are responsible for causing a lot of trouble. They ride in on any negativity so that problems are exaggerated. They interfere with what people are hearing and so cause misunderstanding. They use people's insecurities and self-defences against them. They do all they can to hinder the love and unity that are crucial in the Church if we are to forbear with one another, be understanding and compassionate towards one another, and help one another remain free from the influences of darkness.

It is important not to become fearful with insights such as these but to thank God for them because He offers the way in which to stop such interference from the enemy. If we ask, God will always alert us to the hidden work of the enemy so that we can cooperate with Him in stopping the enemy's schemes and in freeing people from his darkness. This is an important aspect of intercession not only for those who have yet to come to faith but also on behalf of those who are affected by any evil spirits within the body of Christ.

Recently, when I was praying, I was shown a picture of an octopus lying lazily on a beach. It appeared to be sleeping and was fairly well camouflaged by the sand but its arms were occasionally shooting out and trying to draw in chosen prey. As I watched, it was targeting me but couldn't touch me. I was fascinated as this was at a time when I was struggling with extreme lethargy for no obvious reason. Once I saw the picture, I realised that the spirit of Ahab was affecting me but not able to capture me. I was encouraged.

Chapter 2:8

The Realm of Jezebel

"Nevertheless, I have this against you: You tolerate that woman Jezebel, who calls herself a prophet. By her teaching she misleads my servants into sexual immorality and the eating of food sacrificed to idols."
Revelation 2:20

The spirits in the Realm of Jezebel display arrogancy and demand subservience. They may be present in men or women. As it is often generational it may affect a person in a similar way to a familiar spirit. It waits for its chance to strike at a time of trauma, shock, anger or rejection. Scripture records Jezebel as introducing her gods into Israel through inviting the prophets of Baal and Asherah to dine with her at her table. She ordered the extermination of all the prophets of the Lord.[126] The four clusters of spirits within the stronghold of Jezebel are seductiveness, control, conniving and flattery.

Anyone who is influenced by a Jezebel spirit may display only a few of the many possible characteristics which I now describe. People may think that the traits of a Jezebel spirit apply more to women than to men but either can be affected. This spirit has the ability to creep into situations or into people's lives and take them unawares. In the book

---

126 1 Kings 18:1-19.

of Revelation, she is depicted as the temptress who tempts others towards anything that is not of God.

Jezebel spirits are religious but cloak themselves with "spirituality" and "intellectualism". Their obsession is for rulership, authority and control. They have a desire to appear more spiritual than others, and so may give false teaching rather than the true food of the Word of God.[127] Messages given by a person under the control of a Jezebel spirit may intimidate, confuse, cause fear, inadequacy, self-defensiveness, or fuel self-pity. Those under the influence of such spirits are quick to offer help but, because of their need to control, often disempower others, making them feel inferior and inadequate.

These spirits want to be the centre of attention and as such, may encourage soulish prophecy, perhaps using God's name to further their cause or "prophesying" known facts as though they received them directly from God, perhaps "prophesying" what a person wants to hear, or perhaps receiving insights from other demons. This last source is the practice of divination.[128] The Jezebel spirit targets true prophets of God in an attempt to stop the message of God from opening eyes so that its own deceptive ways cannot be seen. Because it hates the prophetic voice, it tries to hinder this through confusion and thereby cause a person hearing God to question whether it really is God's voice. It targets those full of the Holy Spirit and who are increasing in the anointing of God, by trying to stop their efficacy through sucking out the life of God.

Those affected by Jezebel spirits may seek to control leaders and like to have an exclusive relationship with the pastor of a church. They have no regard for Godly authority and will try to usurp such authority with lies, distortions and soulish prayers, for example, praying, "Father, show the pastor the deeper things you are showing us". The

---

127 Revelation 2:20.
128 Ezekiel 12:24; 13:1-23; Jeremiah 23:9-14.

story of Jezebel with regard to Naboth illustrates well her scheming to destroy a person's character and identity and so stop them from achieving their destiny which in the case of Naboth was to care for his ancestral vineyard.[129]

They give the impression that they have at heart the good of everyone else rather than of themselves, and can be seen as "do-gooders". They manoeuvre themselves into places of authority where they can target others to do their evil work while coming alongside to offer "godly" help. They woo others with flattery, false acceptance and graciousness, lulling them into passivity, while they themselves seek constant affirmation. All the time they are working towards achieving a position of pre-eminence. Those whom they target may be deceived into believing that they are serving God. They get entry through people's self-centredness, immaturity or woundedness and, if anyone does not do what they want, a pressure beyond reason will be applied to manipulate and control. The person under the sway of a Jezebel spirit keeps others in fellowship with them but does not like them to fellowship with each other in their absence. If anyone belonging to their group is not present for any reason, they will follow that person up and ask why so as to ascertain whether that person is breaking free from their control and fleshly appetite. If they do not get their own way, they may become angry or behave in some other ungodly way. The fruit of the Spirit is absent and, instead, the person dominated by such a spirit walks according to the flesh.

One of their aims is to lead God's servants astray and beguile them into idolatry through goals like materialism and love of money.

They use Godly things for ungodly purposes. These spirits may target an individual or even a whole church, enticing them into practising

---

129 1 Kings 21.

sexual vice.[130] When confronted they use a seductive voice,[131] which can be amusing. Certain aspects of this spirit such as the sexual are behind adultery, manipulation, and betrayal. Not only do they encourage physical sexual fornication but also use the spiritual form to lure people away from their true Spiritual covering. They cause church splits and broken marriages and friendships, with the intention of spoiling lives.

Those who have adopted a lifestyle dominated by a Jezebel spirit can be almost irresistible, charismatic and sensitive, causing others to feel guilty if they speak out in negative assessment. If it suits their purposes, they will betray someone whom they have befriended.

They are jealous and if a person has something that they want they will stop at nothing to try and get it. They are defensive, self-righteous, nosey, and gossips. They accuse, misrepresent, are insubordinate and full of pride, while portraying false humility. They are resentful and bitter, vindictive without mercy, and may assassinate a person's character, perhaps using witchcraft to take revenge. If a Jezebel spirit has gained entry in a person through past woundedness and consequent shutting down of part of their heart, then it can affect the emotions and thereby make it difficult for anyone to rationalise with them.

These spirits rebel against God by using all three aspects of witchcraft: manipulation, domination and intimidation. They can cause fatigue and sickness in the body, and provoke fear in the mind and heart as well as foster sorrow, regrets, hopelessness, loneliness, darkness, depression and fear of death.

The spirit of Jezebel in a person works with the spirit of Ahab in a person of the other gender,[132] as exemplified by King Ahab who was

---

130 Revelation 2:22-23.
131 Revelation 2:20,22.
132 1 Kings 16:29-33.

weak-minded[133] and allowed himself to be led by his wife Jezebel so as to suit his own purposes.[134] Ahab spirits stir up those with Jezebel spirits who are self-righteous and judgemental. The spirit needs to be severed from all sources of strength such as other spirits, and any "puppet strings" cut. It doesn't like mention of the Blood of Jesus as this means death to it. The Jezebel spirit is a strongman whose house needs to be spoiled before it will go.[135] Once this is done, it is actually quite weak and powerless and leaves without a fuss.

When ministering to someone who has a Jezebel spirit, we need to be aware that the Jezebel spirit may fire darts at the one ministering, who may then become discouraged and low in mood. We can guard against this through praying for protection and, if we are affected, we can ask Jesus to remove any such darts together with their effects and consequences.

As in all ministry to a person love is the key for demons hate love. Only as someone with this spirit is affirmed as a person and loved unconditionally can they be helped to recognise what is happening. Inner healing and healing from brokenness may be required before a person recognises the influence of this spirit. Repentance and subsequent deliverance ensure that the person enters into a secure place in the knowledge of God's love for them and is enabled to sense that they belong to the family of God.

---

133 1 Kings 21:4.
134 1 Kings 21:7, 25.
135 Matthew 12:29.

Chapter 2:9

The Realm of Witchcraft

"There shall not be found among you anyone who makes his son or his daughter pass through the fire, or one who practices witchcraft, or a soothsayer, or one who interprets omens, or a sorcerer, or one who conjures spells, or a medium, or a spiritist, or one who calls up the dead."
Deuteronomy 18:10-11

The spirits in the Realm of Witchcraft use witchcraft which is a form of satanic power, an attribute of satan. They frequently occur alongside Jezebel spirits. The four clusters of spirits within the stronghold of Witchcraft are rebellion, control, mockery and sickness.

Witchcraft is rebellion against God and occurs when we deliberately move in witchcraft practice or choose to go our own way in defiance of God's will no matter how well we rationalise it to ourselves,

"For rebellion is like the sin of divination, and arrogance like the evil of idolatry. Because you have rejected the word of the Lord, he has rejected you as king." 1 Samuel 15:23

Any occult practice and the influence of witchcraft spirits can prevent a person from fully maturing in Christ and produce an atmosphere of darkness and fear. Witchcraft is rife in our society and is the religion of fallen man using different forms to achieve control. It is evil and counterfeits God-given spirituality.

As children in God's kingdom, we regard witchcraft as ungodly, and so it is, but even we can be unintentionally guilty of it. For example, when we read and believe our horoscopes or go to a fortune teller, we are looking to someone or something other than God to enlighten us. Because the source of that knowledge is evil, we are in danger of submitting to some sort of demonic control over our life. Words given often cause fear or false expectancy. Unintentional witchcraft can also occur when a person is bitter and resentful towards another and unknowingly curses that person in their hearts. It can occur when a parent dominates a family to such an extent that the children rebel or it can interfere in marital relationships.

The Holy Spirit never controls because God has chosen to give each of us freedom of will. It is our choice to submit to God. The good news is that when we do, no matter how deeply involved we have been in witchcraft, we are forgiven and can be restored in Jesus' name.

Legalism, trusting in the flesh, manipulation, intimidation and domination all have their roots in witchcraft. Mainly through curses and spells, witchcraft spirits can impose emotions, behaviours or circumstances upon people that they would not otherwise have. These spirits have three main foci: to alter the forces of nature, for example, through "rainmakers"; to alter the course of life, for example, in the ability to bring forth children (fertility); and to control human beings. Witchcraft, sorcery, divination and consulting the spirits are all different forms of witchcraft control,

> *"Do not turn to mediums or seek out spiritists, for you will be defiled by them. I am the Lord your God."* Leviticus 19:31

Witchcraft (black magic) is the power element of control. It includes curses, personal domination, hexes etc. Black magic witchcraft works directly with satan and takes place through many means: sacrifices including that of humans, oaths, covenants, curses, spells, incantations, telekinesis, potions, drugs, and music. Using music, the witchcraft doctor's aim is to get his tribe so full of demons that they will win the battle. Sorcery (red magic) uses things and objects to control, for example, amulets, charms, music, dancing etc. The use of demonic imprints[136] can be used to give a foothold in a person's life, and the use of dolls as effigies or of clothes can facilitate cursing. Divination (white magic) uses activities like fortune telling, revelation, tarot cards, tea-cup reading to control. Spiritism uses knowledge from an evil source and consultation with evil spirits to control, and is used especially in healing. God is against all practice of witchcraft.[137]

Witchcraft is widely used, sometimes deceptively hidden by a false "christian" veneer,

- to display healings

- to give prophesies

- to offer quick remedies and certainties

- to give people what they ask for

- to cause calamities, curses, illness etc.

Because of lack of knowledge people sometimes accept and use these without realising it is witchcraft.

The use of curses was highlighted earlier in chapter 2.2. Another example was uncovered when a lady and her daughter came for help.

136 Our Victory over Evil, Chapter 2.2.
137 Deuteronomy 18:9-15.

As we prayed, we received the revelation that they were being crushed as the result of the effects of a curse that had been passed down through several generations from a time when parents had rejected their daughter because she had given birth to a child out of wedlock. Because God has chosen not to control people, He had to allow this curse even though its effects that could have crushed every first child in each generation. However, He had restricted it in intensity, using it to strengthen both the lady and her daughter. Each had remained strong in their faith in Jesus and not been crushed as the enemy intended. Once the presence of the curse was recognised, we were able to free the lady and her daughter from its effects and influences in Jesus' name. This was an example of how even when there is a foothold for a curse to land and to be repeated, God may intervene and restrict the frequency and/or the strength of the curse.

There are different types of curses and many ways of releasing a person from them e.g.,

- a single curse sent by one person against one person. In Jesus' name we sever the person from the curse together with its influences and effects, cut the ungodly soul and spirit ties linking the two people returning to each what belongs to them, and remove any spirit associated with the curse. We then ask God to heal the person from its effects.

- a two-fold curse is one that is split two ways to affect two people. We sever between the two aspects of the curse in Jesus' name and then pray as above for each person.

- a compound curse occurs when several people each send the same curse against one person. The separate curses are combined and sent as one strong curse. In this case we sever between the people sending the curses, sever between the curses together with their influences and effects, and then sever the person from each and every curse together with its influences and effects and command the curse to lose momentum, all in Jesus' name. We then ask God to heal the person from the effects and influences of the curse.

- concentric curses round a person are where curses are sent by a more than one coven, person etc., and are not joined together. Each can be dismantled in turn as detailed previously.

- curses can be sent against a person through using an object belonging to them. We can ask for an angel to stand between the person who is sending a curse and the owner of the object, and cleanse it with the Blood of Jesus.

- a curse can be put into effect through using effigies of a person. In Jesus' name we sever between the person being afflicted and the effigies of them, and disassociate them from the effigies praying as before.

- caging and then cursing a person leads to the person feeling more of what they already feel, for example, feeling worthless.

- curse of the "word" (satan's book). As well as curses that come from people via the demonic, there are curses that come from satan via the demonic and which are from the Black Mass Book. Using the words from this to bring curses on people is the antetype to using God's Word to bless people. Such curses are very strong and often cannot be shifted by the usual forms of prayer but by the Word of God,

"You shall not touch My anointed one nor do My prophets any harm." 1 Chronicles 16:22

If someone is practising witchcraft against another, we can pray a safeguard over their mind, heart and spirit and that God will surround and bathe them in His love. Whenever we come across curses in any form it is wise for us to seek God for His way of dealing with it.

Witchcraft in scripture

In the Acts of the Apostles, we read that seven exorcists were copying what they had heard Paul say but, because they didn't have a relationship with Jesus, they were using His name without His authority. The consequences were serious,

> *"Some Jews who went around driving out evil spirits tried to invoke the name of the Lord Jesus over those who were demon-possessed. They would say, 'In the name of the Jesus whom Paul preaches, I command you to come out.' Seven sons of Sceva, a Jewish chief priest, were doing this. One day the evil spirit answered them, 'Jesus I know, and Paul I know about, but who are you?' Then the man who had the evil spirit jumped on them and overpowered them all. He gave them such a beating that they ran out of the house naked and bleeding."* Acts 19:13-16

However, God brought good out of the situation: believers responded to what they had seen, burning their occult books out of fear, and the name of the Lord Jesus was magnified as seen in Acts 19:17.

In Acts 8 we read that the people of Samaria had been deceived by sorcery until they heard the good news but that on hearing it, they and the sorcerer believed and were baptised,

> *"Now for some time a man named Simon had practiced sorcery in the city and amazed all the people of Samaria. He boasted that he was someone great, and all the people, both high and low, gave him their attention and exclaimed, 'This man is rightly called the Great Power of God.' They followed him because he had amazed them for a long time with his sorcery. But when they believed Philip as he proclaimed the good news of the kingdom of God and the name of Jesus Christ, they were baptized, both men and women. Simon himself believed and was baptized. And he followed*

Philip everywhere, astonished by the great signs and miracles he saw." Acts 8:9-13

Another example in scripture is recorded in Galatians. After the Galatians had been baptised and filled with the Spirit[138] Paul learnt that a false gospel had been brought to them which had led their returning to their former witchcraft ways.[139] He asked them,

"Who has bewitched you?" Galatians 3:1

All through Old and New Testament we read about satan's influence in driving people into practising of the occult but the good news is that he has been defeated in that realm at the cross.

Witchcraft can imitate infirmities and through the power of suggestion lead people to believe they are truly ill. Several years ago, I had pain that seemed like arthritis in my left hand but when I asked God about it, I was given the impression that it was caused by witchcraft and so I rebuked the spirit of witchcraft. After six months of steadily refusing to believe it was arthritis and consistently rebuking the spirit my hand felt free of pain. A year later a similar pain again affected my left hand but I was prepared this time and when I rebuked the spirit the pain left immediately. If I had believed this lie from witchcraft, it could have led to me giving a foothold for a spirit of arthritis to enter and thereby increase any disability. Jezebel also can use her power of suggestion to gain access for a spirit of infirmity to take up residence.

Since witchcraft is a power source and afraid of losing its power the spirit of deception may be used to camouflage it so that deliverance from witchcraft is hindered. Sometimes Jesus allows this to continue for a while during a period of ministry so as to lure the enemy into a false sense of security.

---

138 Galatians 1:6-9.
139 Galatians 1:6-9.

It is never the will of God for one person to dominate another. This is soulish rather than spiritual,

> *"But if ye have bitter envying and strife in your hearts, glory not, and lie not against the truth. This wisdom does not descend from above, but is earthly, soulish, demonic."* James 3:14-15

> *"Because the carnal mind is enmity against God; for it is not subject to the law of God, nor indeed can be. So then, those who are in the flesh cannot please God."* Romans 8:7-8

"Earthly, soulish, demonic"— this is the order of degeneration. What begins as earthly and soulish can lead to evil spirits attaching to or using it. The spirit of witchcraft fears holiness, i.e., obedience to and following God. Holiness doesn't curse but blesses. A person who is moving in holiness is prepared to wait for God's timing and comes to God with no pre-conditions. Such a person never uses manipulation or attempts to control circumstances but has a simple and faithful trust in the goodness of God.

Chapter 2:10
The Realm of Idolatry

"You should have the same attitude toward one another that Christ Jesus had, who though he existed in the form of God did not regard equality with God as something to be grasped, but emptied himself by taking on the form of a slave, by looking like other men, and by sharing in human nature. He humbled himself, by becoming obedient to the point of death – even death on a cross!"
Philippians 2:5-8

The Realm of Idolatry establishes itself around and within us whenever we open ourselves up to spirits of idolatry by setting our hearts on anything other than God. Such distractions take from us what should be offered to God, and our worship becomes focussed away from God. Scripture teaches,

> *"Love the Lord your God with all your heart, with all your soul, with all your strength, and with all your mind, and love your neighbour as yourself."* Luke 10:27

Through strongly held desires our hearts can be drawn away from a God-focus onto something else: a person, our own false beliefs, possessions, ungodly ideologies, political or social systems etc. At a time when God was healing my heart, He revealed to me that I had some wrong beliefs because of my background learning and experience. This was idolatry. Good theology is where man's understanding of scripture and revelation by the Spirit are in harmony. The four clusters of spirits within the stronghold of Idolatry are fornication, arrogance, backbiting and jealousy.

We are called to,

> *"Humble yourselves, therefore, under God's mighty hand, that he may lift you up in due time."* 1 Peter 5:6

God looks for people who in humility accept His authority. Idolatry is deception and once we open the door, we open ourselves to further deception.

There are many types of idolatry. Obvious idolatry occurs when a person knows that they are submitting themselves to the powers behind idols. This may be because they have not heard of Jesus and, in ignorance, are worshipping other gods. Members of various sects and cult religions may be deceived. Some church-goers may idolise their leaders or a charismatic personality. Within our personal lives there may be something that takes up an excessive amount of time thus denying us fellowship with God. Materialism is a form of idolatry. Getting things out of balance, perhaps in relationships, as with husbands and wives or parents with children, can be a form of idolatry. There can be those who put love of and knowledge of scripture before relationship with God and use it to throw "hand grenades" wherever they go. This is idolatry. Jesus warned us,

> *"You study the Scriptures diligently because you think that in them you have eternal life. These are the very Scriptures that testify about me, yet you refuse to come to me to have life"*. John 5:39-40

Some, when called into a ministry, think more of the ministry than of the God of the ministry. This is idolatry. We can have religious idolatry inside the church, for example, fanaticism about a specific denomination being the one with absolute truth, unwillingness to change worship practices, adherence to the status quo, holding on to sacred theological cows, pride in position, doing things from habit rather than as a consequence of godly vision. As has been said, "change is here to stay". We can even be worshipping a "god" that has been manufactured in our minds. Let us be diligent in listening to our own hearts with our spiritual antennae, in listening to our preferences and beliefs and our good ideas, and in checking these with what we hear by listening to the Spirit of Jesus while reading the scriptures.

In scripture, we find that idolatry is found alongside deception and beguiling which are characteristics of Antichrist and Witchcraft spirits, seduction which is a characteristic of Jezebel spirits, and subversion and subtlety which are characteristics of Ahab spirits. All evil spirits use their vast plethora of "weapons" to side-track us from our walk with Jesus and so we must be alert and wearing the armour of God.[140]

Idolatry can lead to jealousy and deception as shown in the story of Abraham who was jealous for His wife in her beauty.[141] It can be seen in David's worship of Bathsheba.[142] From these and other examples we see that the pathway of idolatry can lead us into sin.

God desires truth in our inner being. It is Christ in us who reveals truth alongside grace otherwise our truth can become legalism.

---

140 Ephesians 6:18ff.
141 Genesis 12:10ff.
142 2 Samuel 11:2-3.

Our hearts are deceitful and desperately wicked[143] so we need to seek God and ask Him to reveal what is hidden there.[144] In the light of the holiness of God, Isaiah saw himself as he really was.[145] Unless we look to God and see the nature of God, we will not see ourselves through the eyes of truth. When we receive the truth from God, He will cleanse our hearts and put a right spirit within us.[146]As with all sin, the journey out from it begins with allowing Jesus to shine His light in our hearts so that by the grace of God we can recognise it. Humility before Him brings us into repentance and release in Jesus' name, followed by cleansing and consequent freedom. As we walk out of all the deception of idolatry, we are able to walk in truth, seeing and hearing through the eyes of the Spirit of Jesus. We will be envisioned by the Spirit as were Peter, Philip, Paul and many, many others.

One final word to strengthen us. Some worry that if they were put to the test and given an ultimatum that they might deny God. God looks on the heart, and He knows when a person is worshipping Him from their heart, even when they are physically made to bow the knee through persecution. We can and must lean on the mercy and grace of God and recognise that of ourselves we are powerless but in Christ we are full of power, His power.

---

143 Jeremiah 17:9.
144 Psalm 139:24.
145 Isaiah 6:1-8.
146 Psalm 51:10.

Chapter 2:11

The Realm of Death and Hell

"Then Death and Hades were thrown into the lake of fire.
This is the second death – the lake of fire."
Revelation 20:14

The Realm of Death and Hell is the domain in which suffering and loss is perpetuated through the oppression of evil spirits of death and hell. Spirits of death bring loss of life in some aspect and spirits of hell bring torment with it. There are numerous references to King David wrestling with death and hell but being delivered by God.[147] Many people exist in continuous "living hell" because they are under a strongman of death and hell. The four clusters of spirits within the stronghold of death and hell are destruction, division, discouragement and dissension.

Spirits of death and hell can affect life and every aspect of life but people can be free from them by choosing to live life in Jesus. Because our everyday lives have evolved with so many pressures and stresses, it can appear at times that death has more power than it has had previously but this is not the case. We nurture death through ungodly lifestyles, materialism, selfishness, desires and anxieties. Some of

---

147 2 Samuel 22:4-7; Psalm 9:13; 86:13; 116:3-9.

the openings that give such spirits a foothold in people are deep rejection and abandonment, self-mutilation, depression and suicidal tendencies, ungodly covenants, broken covenants, the occult, drug and alcohol abuse and unclean spirits. Spirits of death and hell can give rise to diseases, plagues and infirmities. Spirits of destruction can influence people so that they hear the enemy's voice but mistake it for Jesus' voice because of the accompanying confusion. They can obstruct gifts of healing, miracles and deliverance, hinder the harvest of souls, and blind the people of God to the seasons of God.

Apollyon, or Destruction, is the demonic king of death over the bottomless pit,[148] and a strongman in the realm of death and hell. Evil spirits in this realm aim to destroy, ruin, and decimate causing total loss. There is one Destroyer but many spirits of destruction. In satanism and witchcraft the Destroyer may give demonically controlled groups specific commands that become like harpoons fired over a person and forming a net of curses. If a person is being cursed in this way, then they can free themselves through praying as outlined earlier. They can ask that the cross of Jesus be put between them and those cursing them.

These evil spirits use curses to curtail God's people in their God-given assignments by making them feel tired and worn out to the point of giving up or by giving them sharp pain in the head or stomach so that they are unable to focus on anything else. They can cause breathing problems.

On occasion, a person might even feel they want to die and, perhaps, commit suicide. Generational curses can lead to suicide, early death, accidental death, accidents, sicknesses, mental health issues, repeated miscarriages, breakdown of marriages, continuing financial difficulties, and being accident prone. These spirits bring pressure,

---

148 Revelation 9:11.

affect relationships through distraction and irritation causing people to fight, and they interfere with Godly intentions, sometimes hindering scheduled prayer. They bring guilt and condemnation. Like the other realms, these spirits make suggestions that are lies. Some objects carry a curse with them.[149] Discernment through our spirits reveals the truth. We can ask Jesus to unblock our ears to hear His truth and that He help us to recognise destruction at work. We can ask God to surround us and our homes with His love and His glory to stop destruction interfering.

Dissension mixes up communication. Under the influence of dissension, statements can become twisted in the hearer's mind, and wrong statements can appear to be right. This is important to discern within a Christian setting so that we are not deceived. Sometimes it can be difficult to recognise dissension in a person who has a following so we must be alert to any warning from God. Only the Spirit of God can discern who are truly His and who are not, and only His Spirit can alert us to danger. Accusation, gossip and dissension all lead to death. In Jesus' name we can isolate the Church from the realm of death and hell and from all the effects and influences of division, discouragement, dissension, and destruction. There are many, many ways in which we can pray but God will lead us in His way each time we ask.

In all of this we can see the overlap of, or collaboration between, various realms such as witchcraft, idolatry, and death and hell. Knowing the source of torment in our lives should not be feared as it can reveal the pathway to freedom. As God's children we can free ourselves in Jesus' name because we are in Christ and He has paid the price for the consequences of rebellion. We can pray that God will give His angels charge over us,

---

149 Deuteronomy 7:26.

"For He shall give His angels charge over you, to keep you in all your ways." Psalms 91:11

and we can cover ourselves with the Blood of Christ as protection. It is important to remember that Jesus commanded all to,

"love your enemies, bless those who curse you, do good to those who hate you, and pray for those who spitefully use you and persecute you." Matthew 5:44

The steps we take to be free from spirits of death and hell are similar to those used to evict other spirits. We must repent (choose to turn away from) the sins of our forefathers which brought curses and evil spirits into the family line, and turn to Jesus. We then sever ourselves in Jesus' name from any generational curse together with its influences and effects, and from the spirit behind it, and break its power and command the spirit to leave in Jesus' name. If the spirit is there because of our own sin then we repent and command the spirit to leave in Jesus' name. Finally, in Jesus' name, we cleanse ourselves from the effects and influences and ask Jesus to heal us.

Jesus cried with a loud voice, *"Lazarus, come forth!"* and then said to onlookers, *"Loose him, and let him go."*[150] This is an interesting record because we were told that Jesus commanded Lazarus to come forth, i.e., to arise into life, and then He ordered that the wrappings of death be removed. This event came to mind one time when God healed me from a bad fall. I had fallen out the back door and it seemed to me that I had hit every part of me from head to toe on the paving. I was badly shaken so I hobbled onto a chair and soaked in God's presence, inviting the Holy Spirit to go to every place that was hurting. When I felt better I looked in the mirror to see what damage was done. There wasn't a single bruise anywhere. However, as the day continued my

---

150 John 11:43-44.

ankle became extremely painful so much so that I couldn't put my weight on it and the following day I decided to visit the doctor. After hobbling into the on-call surgery, I was told that I might be put in plaster or even a boot. Having then struggled into the outpatients at the local hospital I sat waiting for my call for an X-ray. When I stood up, the extreme pain had left. I was mystified. The X-ray showed that the ankle wasn't broken and so I was given a support stocking with instructions to wear it for a week. The following day the ankle was weak and I knew that I had to stand for an hour teaching that evening so I spent time with God asking Him to heal it. Once I had prayed and commanded healing in Jesus' name, I heard the words, "take the graveclothes off". I understood this to be referring to the support stocking so I took it off and was able to stand without any pain. I never had another pain in the ankle since.

"O Death, where is your sting? O Hades, where is your victory?"
1 Corinthians 15:55

Jesus often used command to free people, as when he healed the paralysed man, the man with blind eyes, and the one with a deaf and dumb spirit. He commanded Tabitha to arise, the young man in the coffin to awake, and the leper to be clean. We really do need to listen to what God tells us to do when praying for ourselves and for others as often the prayer of command in Jesus' name is needed rather than supplication. As has been said, the Blood of Jesus is the complete antidote to death and hell. In Exodus we read of the night when the destroyer passed over the Israelite households where the Blood of sacrifice had been put over the lintel and the two side posts.[151] This is a shadow of the reality of the power of the Blood of Jesus to keep us safe. It is our responsibility to apply the Blood.

---

151 Exodus 12:23.

When the trappings of death are removed there is peace, life and love. Instead of seeing only sorrow a person sees life and beauty, colours and movement. Life is seen in all its fullness in flowers, trees and shrubs, rivers and streams, oceans, the night sky and the animals. Above all, life is seen in all its beauty in each person, all made in the image of God.

What is called life on earth isn't really life in all its abundance as God intended. In the beginning there was no death nor hell but our sin has allowed it. While we are journeying through this life, we have a choice. Either we embrace Jesus' way or we turn our backs on it and follow the way of death and hell. Passing through death is a reality, something that needs to be faced but not feared by those who have chosen Jesus' way. It is merely death to our bodies but continuing life for our souls and spirits, a brief transition, like saying, "Goodnight, see you in the morning". Those who love Jesus and who live with Him and in Him during their life here on earth will continue in Christ and flow without interruption into life with Him in heaven forever. Death has no hold over us.

Life is knowing Jesus and the power of His resurrection. It is knowing that even when the nights are dark and long or the pain unbearable Jesus is with us offering us grace and mercy, comforting and establishing us in certain hope. Jesus makes the difference. Jesus is life. He gives us life even along the road of suffering. He strengthens and gives us life when we look foolish in the eyes of the world because of following Him.

On the day of Pentecost, the disciples were waiting as commanded for the promise that was to come.[152] We read about the outpouring of the Holy Spirit upon them for witness[153] and, throughout the book of Acts, the effects of that outpouring. They were baptized in fire and

---

152 Acts 1:8; Luke 24:49.
153 Acts 2:1-4, 46-47.

were of one accord, a unity that pulled down strongholds such as we are describing. As with all strongholds, we pray to be free ourselves and that the body of Christ will also be released. There are many scriptures that we can decree and release in our battle against the enemy of Jesus and His church. The Holy Spirit will lead us to do so in God's timing. Then,

> *"we the redeemed shall be strong in purpose and unity declaring aloud praise and glory, wisdom and thanks, honour, and power, and strength be to our God forever and ever."*[154]

---

154 Salvation Belongs to Our God, Crystal Lewis, Exodus, paraphrased.

Chapter 2:12

The Realm of Deception

"Jesus answered them, "You are deceived, because you don't know the scriptures or the power of God."
Matthew 22:29

Within the Realm of Deception there are three aspects, deception, illusion and delusion. Deception is an umbrella word referring to anything false whereas illusion refers to wrong perceptions, and delusion to idiosyncratic beliefs or impressions opposing reality. Spirits of deception may link up with spirits of witchcraft to give death to the senses and deception outside a person can use illusion to deceive. At such a time the illusion can act like a veil and cloud our sight so that we see incorrectly. An example of this occurred when a friend fell down the stairs because she misjudged the height of the handrail. When she prayed about it, she was told that a spirit of deception had used illusion to mislead her. When a spirit of deception is affecting us what we think we see or hear may not always be correct and so dissension may arise between us and others and we become bewildered by any subsequent fall-out. The four clusters of spirits within the stronghold of deception are falsehood, hypocrisy, good works, false worship and false Bible teaching.

In Joshua 7 we read that the Israelites were deceived when they, "... did not inquire of the Lord"[155] but instead sent scouts to survey the size of the enemy army and were defeated at Ai. This endorses how crucial it is to seek God before making important decisions as we can easily be deceived by our own observations. We are also shown in this story that disobedience, stealing, lying, coveting, and taking the enemy's devoted things to put with their own possessions meant that the Israelites could not stand against their enemies,

"Israel has sinned; they have violated my covenant, which I commanded them to keep. They have taken some of the devoted things; they have stolen, they have lied, they have put them with their own possessions. That is why the Israelites cannot stand against their enemies." Joshua 7:11-12

Spirits of deception mislead, exerting pressure on others to come into agreement. It can take many forms through the "clever" use of words and through misleading actions and behaviour and can be almost undetectable e.g., a small lie within a large body of truth. Just as, in fishing, a hook is disguised by a worm so, also, deception like all evil spirits is camouflaged by the presence of some truth. People living with deception portray an extremely generous and thoughtful attitude until they are found out then they thrash about in anger just like a fish does on a hook. Only as we listen to the discernment that God gives us can we be protected from deception.

Deception is extremely subtle and the person influenced by it can become proficient at appearing innocent, at covering up their own shortfalls and at passing blame onto others. They can beguile, so that a person on the receiving end can become caught up in emotion, feeling sympathy or pity, and thereby be drawn into the deception without realising. Pride is kept hidden by offering comfort with platitudes

---

155 Joshua 9:14.

like, "We all make mistakes". A person who walks consistently in deception opens themselves up to a spirit of deception, and will reach a stage in life where they do not recognise the deception within which they are living. This is why God warns us[156] and tells us that liars will not enter heaven.[157] If we are not willing and able to see both sides of a controversy then we can be self-deceived. If we are self-deceived, we may be unable to see things from another's point of view.

In the spiritual world spirits of deception can pretend to be any other evil spirit and thereby double the emotional upheaval in a person. For example, if spirits of fear and deception are each affecting a person, the spirit of deception may imitate the spirit of fear so as to double the fear that the person is experiencing. If, then, only spirits of fear are commanded to leave, the spirit of deception will remain and cause further havoc.

Deception, if believed will veer a person away from truth, and evil then becomes good and good, evil. Even if a spirit of deception is bound that will not stop it from influencing a person if they believe the lie. Our safety is in following God and seeking His discernment. He tells us not to be concerned about such things as He will instruct us as we live in Him and look to Him.

Some of the deceptions held by people are denial of Biblical truths, of the gifts of the Holy Spirit for today, and of the works of the Holy Spirit. Wrong mindsets or belief systems, being guided by feelings rather than the Spirit and through believing false prophecy (divination) all lead to deception. We are to test the spirits to see whether they are from God,

---

156 Leviticus 19:11; 1 Timothy 1:9-10 etc.
157 Revelation 21:8.

"Dear friends, do not believe every spirit, but test the spirits to see whether they are from God, because many false prophets have gone out into the world." 1 John 4:1

We are warned that,

"The Spirit clearly says that in later times some will abandon the faith and follow deceiving spirits and things taught by demons." 1 Timothy 4:1

If we are not alert and watchful, we may not realise when a voice we think is God's is actually the voice from a spirit of deception. If we do not learn to distinguish between our soul and our spirit, we can be deceived into thinking the source of our thoughts is from God when it may be actually from our own minds and hearts. Once we follow a lie, other deceptions can creep in and we become self-deceived. Pride fosters this possibility and makes it difficult for us to acknowledge and receive the truth. We are told to test everything and hold on to what is good[158] and, as we seek God for discernment, He shines light on our self-deceptions and guides us into truth.

A friend has given me permission to include a paraphrase of what she wrote to me concerning the confusion she experienced because she was mistaking the voice of deception for God's voice,

"I had prayed to God a number of times and each time I had bound all deception. The replies I got I thought were from God but after we talked I asked God to show me the truth. I look back over them and I now believe it was deception. As you said because I had gone along with it, it was able to communicate with me.

---

158 1 Thessalonians 5:21.

Most of the things the spirit of deception said were truth or truth twisted but there was no compassion or insight given to help me change. I felt told off. Also, I already knew the things that he was telling me. I felt like saying 'Tell me something I don't know'. Whenever I came away from praying, I felt confused because it was as if God had told me something but He hadn't really told me anything. I felt uneasy as if something wasn't quite right.

I began wondering what I had done wrong and repented of my pride even though I was confused as to what I had done. "God" hadn't told me specifically what I had done wrong. I learnt that the enemy uses generalisations.

I now recognise the difference between deception's voice and God's voice. God gives understanding as well as the truth e.g., one time I had been thinking wrong thoughts, God said to me 'Control your thoughts'. I didn't obey and this led to me getting upset and crying and then losing my temper. The next day God said to me, 'I am teaching you how your thinking affects your emotions and then produces behaviour'. At the same time as God gave me these words, He showed me what I had done. The words and what he showed me gave me an understanding at a heart level. I had heard these words before but God touched my heart with them and gave me an insight, I felt loved and at peace not condemned.

Another occasion was when I had done something wrong, I had repented but I was still feeling bad. God gave me the verse 'As far as the east is from the west that is how far your transgressions are'. God sought to reassure me, and He did. His words went to my heart and I felt peace."

A cloak of deception can be used by satan to impose false feelings like rejection and worthlessness or to mask other demonic such as a power source. At such times the cloak can be removed from the shoulders in the name of Jesus so that truth surfaces. As a consequence, miserable feelings caused by the deception suddenly disappear and any power source present surfaces and can then be evicted.

We can be protected from deception by binding it and commanding it not to interfere or communicate in Jesus' name and by listening to the Holy Spirit so that we don't come into agreement with a lie. Standing firm on the truth of God's word will flush any spirit of deception to the surface and then it can be ordered to leave. Beware, it is deceptive. Let us be people of truth.

There are many, many scriptures whose truths we can declare in our battle against the enemy of Jesus and His Church. It is important that we study God's words and store them in our spirits. This not only builds us up in the truth but also makes us available to the Holy Spirit to bring about change through us. As He leads us in proclaiming God's truth individuals, people-groups and nations can be released out of darkness and into the light of God.

Epilogue

As we have continued on our *Journey of Discovery*, we have explored further the mystery that is, "God in us". We have discovered that because we are His children, He shares His attributes with us so that we are equipped to do His works,

> *"Very truly I tell you, whoever believes in me will do the works I have been doing, and they will do even greater things than these, because I am going to the Father. And I will do whatever you ask in my name, so that the Father may be glorified in the Son. You may ask me for anything in my name, and I will do it."[159]*

We have affirmed the truth that in Christ we rule in the heavenly places far above all evil principalities and powers[160] and consequently can be free from all attempted enslavement by satan. Jesus said,

> *"If you hold to me teaching, you are really my disciples. Then you will know the truth and the truth will set you free."[161]*

In this life we can indeed soar in freedom.

---

159 John 14:12-14.
160 Ephesians 1:21; 2:6.
161 John 8:32.

Some birds live in cages [162]
They never learn to fly
And like those birds,
I never found my wings
But Lord, your love released me
So I could see the sky
And now my heart rejoices as I sing

Spirit Wings,
You lift me over all
the earth bound things
And like a bird,
my heart is flying free
I'm soaring on the song
your spirit brings
O Lord of all,

You let me see
A vision of,
your majesty
You lift me up
And carry me on your spirit wings

Now when I'm feeling lonely
I just look at You
And soon my heart is soaring high above
Everything is clearer
From Your point of view
Lifted up on spirit wings of love

---

162 Spirit Wings, Album Spirit Wings, Joni Eareckson, Word Music,1982.

The Journey Continues

In the third and final book in this trilogy we will be sharing some insights given by our heavenly Father into various ways in which trauma and broken-heartedness can affect us, and how release and healing can be received. As King Nebuchadnezzar said,

> "Surely your God is the God of gods and the Lord of kings and a revealer of mysteries, ... " Daniel 2:47

God alone knows the intricacies of the human soul and how to guide us out of confusion and turmoil into peace and rest. He alone can heal us so that we enjoy abundant life in Him.[163] He is our Shepherd, leading us into green pastures and beside still waters, restoring our soul.[164] He wants to enjoy companionship with us as we journey through this life towards our heavenly home. He truly is our wonderful heavenly Father who loves us deeply.

---

163 John 10:10.
164 Psalm 23:1.

Contact The Author

office@MinistryoftheFathersHeart.com

Visit our website to learn more
www.MinistryoftheFathersHeart.com

Inspired To Write A Book?

Contact
Maurice Wylie Media
Your Inspirational Christian Publisher

Based in Northern Ireland and distributing around the world.

www.MauriceWylieMedia.com